100 THINGS EVERY BLACK GIRL SHOULD KNOW

for girls 10-100

TAURA STINSON

100 Things Every Black Girl Should Know

Copyright © 2017 by Taura Stinson for EAT WRITE HEAR LLC.

ALL RIGHTS RESERVED

ISBN-13: 978-0692914830

Official Website: www.TauraStinson.com

Cover Art and Chapter Illustrations: Adah Glenn
www.AfroPuff.biz

Editor: Stacey Debono / sdebonoediting@gmail.com

This book is dedicated to three of the most important women in my life
- my mother Yvonne Stinson, my sister Tanecia Stinson,
and our grandmother, Annie Grace Stinson.

Additionally, this book was written in memory of my late grandmother
Mittie Lee Morton, and my aunt Vanessa Dean Williams.

TABLE OF CONTENTS

Introduction

I have been writing this book in my head since High School. I transferred to a different school and became close friends with a group of girls that ALL went to college, but outside of a short stint at junior college, I didn't go. I was no slacker by any means, but when I found out the cost of college, I centered my focus on my other passion - songwriting. In a perfect world, I was going to graduate from UC Berkeley, become a journalist, travel the world and write stories about the beautiful people in it but in my mind, that would mean that I would force my mom into poverty. I wasn't aware of the countless resources that were available to me, so while everyone was applying to college, I was grinding hard in the recording studio. See, my experience was different from that of my high school peers. I was raised in East Oakland. Not the gentrified Oakland that has ascended to one of the nation's most expensive rental markets, but the Oakland that my mother tried her best to protect me from, starting from the time we arrived from Alabama when I was 3 years old. The juxtaposition was crazy then; beautiful beaches, remnants of the Black Panther Movement, torrential crime in the lower bottoms or flats, and of course the palatial, almost pristine Oakland Hills…that's where I went to high school.

Skyline High School is perched at the very top of the Oakland skyline, surrounded by massive mansions as well as modest but utterly dope upper middle-class abodes. In contrast, my first high school, Fremont, was completely different. To put it into perspective, Tom Hanks went to Skyline and Too Short went to Fremont. No shade, painting the picture. After a grueling year at Fremont, my mom found someone who allowed us to use their address in order for me to attend Skyline because I was outside of the district. I kicked and screamed because part of me loved my school, especially the creative writing teacher, Michael Jackson, but the other eighty percent knew that the rest of my time would be filled with fighting, and scared out of my mind like I was in junior high school, so I drew the line in the sand and relented to my mother's request. SNAPS FINGERS!

And just like that, I went from being the girl who thought she was too cute, or the girl who got jumped by nine people in junior high, or the weird girl with the big chest to being invisible; I absolutely loved it! Waking up earlier to make it all the way up that hill was brutal, but the air was different. I felt safe. I was no longer being relentlessly bullied or taunted and I could be as weird as I wanted to be because there were far more weirdos than me up there; that's when I had the epiphany about this book, not this title, but the seed was planted. I started observing how vastly different my peers were at Fremont than those at Skyline. For the most part, we were all young black girls who resided in the same city, but the socioeconomic divide had us in two different mindsets. The conversation at Fremont was largely about "making it", "getting by", and "having babies" while college was the centered focus at Skyline, but I already made up my mind. I wasn't going to college; instead, I would become a successful songwriter. Oh, if I only knew how hard that would be. Or if I only knew that applying myself in school would have made it possible for me to even go to college for free.

SMH. *Coulda. Woulda. Shoulda.*

It didn't help that my new friends at Skyline, except for maybe one, were from two-parent, upwardly mobile homes. It was the first time that I heard of Cotillion or Jack & Jill, The Links, and so many other things that baffled me. I would often listen long enough to catch on, and then go to the library and look things up. This was well before the almighty Google, and all that research opened my mind up to the infinite possibilities that awaited me.

Once, I visited with an old friend with whom I attended Fremont. She was raised by a single mother too, but much different than mine. In my house, if school let out at 3:05, I needed to be home by 3:30, period. My mom wasn't playing, and rightfully so. Crack cocaine invaded Oakland in 1984 and my neighborhood seemed to be the first area devastated by it. I remember praying that my mom wouldn't start looking like the 'others'. The 'others' were these beautiful women who I wanted to be just like when I grew up, but when you saw them two weeks later, things had drastically changed for the worse. As a child, however, I was only just getting to know about my mom's strength and resilience that has now become a part of me. But I digress, the friend that I visited had a very specific dream that I cannot share because I would hate for anyone other than her to know that this is about her. Anyway, the dream that she had for her future would require her to get an associate degree and I supported her in this quest while we were growing up. Even though her career path was one less traveled, I was so motivated by the fact that she had a clear goal in mind. But during this particular visit, she had given up on it. In just the 11th grade, before real adult life even started, she had given up and somehow, I was devastated. The thing is, she became absolutely what she told me that she would become at her apartment that day and without further divulging anything, I will say that her dream died inside of her and now she has children whose dreams are dying inside of them too.

I walked away thinking that what we do every day affects our reflection of who we are and who we can become. She was surrounded by girls that weren't motivated and she became less motivated as a result. In that moment, I realized that what my Mom always said is true, "Association brings assimilation" and although I had all kinds of love for my hood, I had to be careful with who I surrounded myself with if I wanted a healthy and successful future.

But believe me, it's easier said than done sometimes, and really hard if you are faced with scrutiny, but guess what? Someone will always be unhappy with your choices, but as long as that someone is not you, you will be just fine.

I unknowingly gained this perspective from my mom. When crack became an epidemic and it was apparent that we were caught in the crossfire, she made sure that I was as far away from it as possible. We couldn't afford to move from Oakland; in fact, I am not sure that she even wanted to. Part of me feels like seeing my people so broken started a fire in me even at that young age, but she got me out of there every chance that she could. Just about every weekend, I would either be in San Ramon at my Auntie Frankie's house or helping my Mom. I don't know how San Ramon is now, but then it was the antithesis of Oakland. My Uncle Boobie was the pastor of our church and even though my cousins and I had our share of mischievous behavior, we were still kids, safe from stray bullets, the allure of fast money, getting high, and crime. When I wasn't in San Ramon, I was assisting my mom with her clients. I washed and blow-dried hair or removed the curl rods from Jheri Curls. If I wasn't there, I was dressed in a super hot Minnie Mouse, Cookie Monster or Big Bird costume, and by hot, I don't mean "fly". I mean hot as in a scalding temperature. My mom's second job was also entrepreneurial; a children's party company called "Joyful Celebrations". If she committed me to a party, that pretty much took up my entire Saturday, and every Sunday was all about church. First Sunday school, then main service, Sunday dinner, and sometimes evening service. I also had to go to church on Tuesday's and Thursday's too. Then there was Birmingham, the birthplace of my parents and me. I spent the third grade there at Council Elementary when my parents first separated and just about every summer, Christmas break or special occasion. The point that I am making is that I didn't have the free time that so many young people have now, and I am so thankful for it because so many of my classmates or neighbors in East Oakland are either dead, in jail, on drugs, living in poverty or worse, still locked inside the prison of their minds.

It really all starts in the mind. You become the best or worst of what you believe you will be and this I know for sure, so instead of talking about the change that I wanted to see, I decided to actually heed the call and write this book. It has been scary, daunting, challenging, and oh, did I say scary? But a necessity. When you hear something, a voice tugging at your spirit and you don't answer, the person that pays the consequences is your self. I have ignored that voice far too many times, but this time I was obedient and my deepest desire is that anyone that picks up this book learns something that they will then pass on to someone else, creating a cycle of awareness. I want the pages to be adorned with spilled beverages, ripped edges, highlighted sections, and underlines. I want little black girls to grow up with this book, referencing certain chapters at pivotal times in their lives. Ideally, it will be updated so that it parallels the times and generations to come; I want us to be better, always.

I want for our narrative to no longer be synonymous with anything other than pride, greatness, and wellness. I want my inner-city girls that never dreamed that they could afford college to find their hope here and pass it along, sparking a wildfire of cultural pride, self-esteem, self-awareness, and self-improvement. At the very same time, I want black women to use this book as a refresher course on both woman and sisterhood. I want a black girl to reference this book as she is sitting in the Oval Office, serving as the first black female POTUS.

I want for us to really "get it". Even those with designer shoes, multiple degrees, head wraps, dread locks, virgin bundles, and successful or impending business women – we all need to be reminded to value ourselves.

Miss me with pomp and circumstance and really carve into the thick of who you are. It takes time and dedication, so roll up your sleeves and let the excavation begin. The 55-year old woman sitting on her couch thinking that life is over needs to know that life as we know it doesn't stop until the heart does, and as long as you have a heart beat, you can affect change in your life and in the lives of others. I need for the millennials to know that their worth is not determined by how many likes or follows they get on social media, or even in real tangible life for that matter. The internal thumbs up is all that matters.

The subtitle, *For Girls 10-100*, was just a clever way of addressing little black girls and the proverbial little black girl inside of us that never learned certain lessons. It's never too late, until it's too late. When "too late" does comes along, my hope and prayer is that you have left behind a rich legacy of love, knowledge, and history that resonates with generations to come.

I have been cautioned about the title of this book. Some asked why didn't I just name it *'100 Things Every Girl Should Know'*. Well, frankly, I am black and the sentiments, experiences, struggles, and victories shared in this book speak to that experience but that does not mean that I don't value the lives of ALL races. It just feels imperative that someone starts the conversation that changes the narrative associated with US.

We are more likely to die of breast cancer, more likely to go to college but less likely to be paid equally in comparison to both men and white women. We are more likely to be affected by domestic violence, most likely to die of heart attacks. That is why this book was written by us, for us. It's time to change the narrative and we can't change it unless we know how.

The "things that you should know" in this book may be things you already know, refuse to acknowledge, or just need to be reminded about; all of it is not exclusive to the black experience but it's my hope that a conversation is started between daughters and mothers, and that a little girl is given this book for her tenth birthday, loves the pictures and sees the beauty in her dark chocolate skin and refers to the vagina chapter if someone touches her in a wrong way when she is 11, or when she's 16 and someone touches her in the right way.

DON'T GASP! This is real life and what you hide will find your children at school or in other social situations. If your girls listen to mainstream radio, believe me, they are ready for this book even if they are six years old. That's for you to decide, just don't turn a blind eye. Twerking will one day go out like the Bump, but something else more suggestive and sexual is likely to land in it's place and at least that's mostly a solo effort; take a cruise around Google and see how "close" our youth are getting when they dance. Once you see that, maybe you will pass this book out to your classroom, youth group, and even to your own children.

I grew up a church girl and there was more freaking going on behind closed doors than at school, so don't think that your "lifestyle" will protect your girls from the inevitable. They have hormones, feelings, desires, and you cannot pray or beat it out of them. The more open and understanding you are, the less likely they are to hide things from you. *You*, whether you're their mother, sister, aunt, guardian, friend, relative or father. Whoever you are to a young impressionable black girl, be sure to pour love, encouragement, and knowledge into their lives.

If you are under 21 and reading this per happenstance or at your own doing, you are already off to a great start. I can only imagine who I would be had I started reciting mantras every day, or if I was pledging allegiance to myself and my community every morning instead of to the flag of the United States of America. I know that pledge by heart and I stand on the principles of it because I was programmed to, even though we are evidence that there isn't in fact, "liberty and justice for all". I'd put my hand over my heart and say it every day in elementary school, and it's still with me. Imagine if you recite the Black Girl Pledge every day. We know that the United States flag is a national monument to be revered, respected, and valued. What if we viewed ourselves in the same way?

When I was a little girl, I played with white Barbies for the most part and more than likely because that was what was accessible to my mom. She worked hard as a beautician and even though we were poor, I never knew it. I ate well, dressed well, and birthdays and Christmas were filled with any and everything that I wanted, and what I "wanted" was what was being advertised to me. As I write this, I hope that there is an advertising executive reading this book who decides to level the playing field when it comes to commercials and print ads. Noted, it's much better than it used to be, but far from what society really looks like. African American or black dolls shouldn't be a niche market that we have to sift through like needles in haystacks. It's imperative that we see ourselves as beautiful and empowered as young adults. When I was little, the Barbie with roller skates or cool Corvette didn't come "black". Again, I know that's changing, but one day I would love to see toys that really reflect society: Black, Asian, Middle Eastern, Indian, Native American, and Hispanic dolls, dolls in wheelchairs, dolls with short hair, alopecia, vitiligo, wider hips, curves...you get the idea.

Visualization of our future selves starts at such a young age and if we are not represented, the seed of discontentment starts to grow. Nip that weed in the bud and buy diverse dolls, toys and books for your children. Please see the Resource Center for a few very cool options.

In fact, the Resource Center in this book is in lieu of a bibliography because I wanted it to feel interesting like a magazine, something that you would actually utilize and view as an extension of the book and not just the back section that nobody reads. The information that I collected via Google is there in the Resource Center as well as in various references made throughout the text. In addition, I include other resources that I am hoping you will enjoy and/or benefit from and for some, never have to use. Feel free to drop me a line if you would like to be included in future updates.

Whew, so... I am excited, nervous, and all kinds of other feelings that I cannot even put into words. I have been a songwriter my entire adult life, having written songs with or for artists, including but not limited to Jennifer Hudson, Mary J. Blige, Destiny's Child, Raphael Saadiq, Cynthia Errivo, Earth Wind & Fire, Steven Tyler of Aerosmith, and Usher. I was an A&R for Music World Entertainment, representing the Sunday Best brand and my first project, *The Awakening of LeAndria Johnson*, garnered a Grammy Award. I was a personal assistant for Paris Hilton and Sean Diddy Combs and worked closely with Dr. Dre, where I got a crash course on life through the eyes of very influential masterminds, yet all of these life experiences pale in comparison to the magnitude of the potential impact of this book.

I have been told that I possess the unique ability to effectively communicate with all walks of life, so my fingers are crossed that this book resonates with you. Let's change our world, one black girl at a time.

Xoxo

Taura Stinson

CHAPTER 1

Mirror Mantras

I didn't realize the power of mantras or positive affirmations until I was in my thirties; this is among the few realizations that led me to writing this book. I thought, "What if I had started this long ago? What if I actually believed in myself when I was 8, 13, or even 20 years old?" I would have been some place off in the stratosphere by now, and although I am grateful for my journey, I do hope that you train your brain to be an optimist, because I wasn't. It's so easy to allow tiny negative seeds to grow into a massive forest of pessimism and before you know it, you are an adult who is desperately trying to find the peace that could have been there all along. Trust me when I say that life is what you make it, so why wait until you are an adult? Now, let's plant seeds on the lush fertile grounds of your heart and soul.

You will need sticky note pads. If you do not have any, grab some tape and paper and if you want to get really creative, grab an erasable marker and head to your mirror. Your mirror may be in your bedroom, bathroom, or closet. If you don't have one, that's okay, you can still participate. I would recommend getting a blank book of any kind and carve out a section specifically for "Mirror Mantras" or if you have the workbook, the section has already been started for you. The most important thing however is to remember that the real mirror is within the soul, and that's where we want the message to live forever.

Write the following ten mantras on your mirror or in your blank book as creatively as you want, as long as you remember to verbalize these affirmations every day. When I wake up in the morning I pray, I affirm, and then I step out into the world. Sometimes I meditate but quite honestly, I am just scraping the surface of that and I am in no position to share any instructions on the matter, but I advocate anything that brings peace and serenity and works for you, however, I understand that not everyone is Christian like me so your processes may be different. These affirmations are not religious or based on any particular faith. These affirmations are for you, for the little girls that want to grow into extraordinary women, and for women who are trying to liberate or validate the little girl inside of them. The goal is to believe in yourself so much that no one can knock you off of your path. This is *your* path and it starts now. No matter where you are, it starts now.

1. I AM BLACK AND I AM PROUD!

It feels good to see the resurgence of pride in and among our people. For so long, we were hung up on being everything but black. People would offer underhanded compliments like, "You are beautiful, what are you mixed with?" but now I see beautiful women and girls of color basking in their blackness and being ever so proud.

2. I AM THANKFUL FOR THIS DAY AND FOR ANOTHER CHANCE TO BE MY ABSOLUTE BEST!

3. I WILL BE WHO I PLAN AND PREPARE TO BE!

This debunks the theory that you can be whoever you want to be. That is a loaded statement. There are few exceptions to the rule, but generally, you MUST plan and prepare. Success happens when opportunity and preparation meet; opportunity means nothing if you are not prepared. Beyonce' wasn't built in a day. She worked hard, even as a young girl, to become the household name that she is today. The same goes for Oprah, First Lady Michelle Obama, Madam CJ Walker, Maya Angelou, Misty Copeland, Alicia Keys; the list could go on forever.8:04 PM The point is, *Success does not grow on trees. The seed must be planted and constantly watered in order for it to bear fruit.*

4. I AM BEAUTIFUL FROM THE INSIDE OUT!

I am keenly aware that my SOUL makes me beautiful. Beauty is not measured in pounds, inches, dollars, pesos, yen, Euros, hair length or textures, eye or skin color, but by integrity, kindness and the ability to love without limits. It's hard these days to remember that beauty isn't something that you can touch with your hands. A kind heart makes one beautiful, not plastic surgery, skin tans, skin lightening, hair weaves or the proverbial fountain of youth. Sure, it's nice to look pretty, but always remember that the soul lives on while the body fades and that's good enough reason to nurture your soul and recognize that it's the light from within that makes us all shine!

5. I DESERVE THE ABSOLUTE BEST THAT LIFE HAS TO OFFER!

My friend and music publisher, Andy, always demands that I get an MFN clause in my contracts. MFN is the acronym for Most Favored Nations, and it basically means that I am to get no less than anyone else. I have since applied this same concept to my life. So often we shrink ourselves to fit into a hole that someone else wants to put us in, but don't shrink! You deserve to go after what you want, in the way that you want, unapologetically. Why? Because you deserve it just as much as the next person!

6. I WILL NOT PUT OFF UNTIL TOMORROW WHAT I CAN DO TODAY!

Lose Wait! No, that is not a typo. The "wait" that I am speaking of is procrastination, a.k.a., THE ENEMY OF PROGRESS. I can tell you this because I have procrastinated so many times and watched my dreams sail right by me, so I urge you to take action. Take your dreams by their wings and fly. So what if you are 12 years old? If you want to go to college, start looking now. Find out what the acceptance criteria is and start working your way toward being ahead of the game. BE PROACTIVE! If you want to be an entrepreneur, why wait until you grow up? At just 13 years old, Asia Newson is Detroit's youngest entrepreneur. Her website is www.SuperBusinessGirl.com and she is selling an assortment of beautiful candles, and guess what? You can be a super business girl too. All that it takes is a dream, planning, and preparation. Jaelyn Bledsoe started an information technology consultancy firm called Bledsoe Technologies when she was 12 years old. By the time she was 16, her firm had grown from two employees to 150 contracted workers, and is reportedly worth $3.5 billion. Yep, my jaw dropped too! But, again, guess what? You can do that too. Meaning you, the teenager, the pre-teen, the 20, 30, 40, 50, 60 or 70, 80 or 90-year old woman reading this right now. You are a success story waiting to happen. Now, I am aware that we don't all have the same resources. I don't know Asia's or Jaelyn's backgrounds, but I do know this: IT STARTS WITH YOU! Your past, your parents and your geographical position in this world will only hinder your success if you allow it to. I do not have all of the answers, but I can tell you to start today. Write out your dream and believe it. google resources in your area. Find yourself a few mentors and follow through. Do not procrastinate. Do not wait. Now is the time to dig deeper.

7. I AM FEARLESS, COURAGEOUS, RIGHTEOUS, AND BRAVE!

8. I AM CONFIDENT, STRONG, AND LOVE MYSELF SO MUCH THAT I DEMAND THE SAME THING FROM ANYONE WANTING TO OCCUPY MY SPACE.

9. I AM A LEADER, AN INNOVATOR, A TRAIL BLAZER, AND A GAME CHANGER!

10. I WILL WATER THE SEED OF GREATNESS PLANTED IN MY SOUL, VISUALIZING WHERE I WILL BE IN THE FUTURE, DAILY!

This one is pretty important for all of us. For instance, I did not graduate college but had I visualized myself going, I probably would have. Instead, I moved to New York and got a record deal while my friends were having the time of their lives; it's one of my biggest regrets. The music business is like a roller coaster ride and unless you are a superstar, it's famine or feast. In other words, sometimes I had an abundance of money while other times, not so much. My cousins in Birmingham, Alabama were all conditioned to go to college, but since my parents and I moved to Oakland when I was three years old, the plan was a little different. My uncle was the pastor of our family church, and marriage was pushed as a rite of passage rather than college. That has worked well for some family members, but I always struggled with it. My first cousin, who was my best friend growing up, was married at 15 years old. I was there in a little chapel in Reno, Nevada wondering "What in the you-know-what is happening?" In retrospect, I know that I was avoiding marriage at all costs. I focused on becoming an "adult" that played by her own rules. I also knew that

I couldn't afford college, so I gave music everything that I had. In hindsight, I see that I could have still done what I loved had I gone to college, and the low points would have been easier to navigate if I had something to fall back on. Yep, news flash, ladies: HAVING MULTIPLE PLATINUM RECORDS IN YOUR ARSENAL DOES NOT MAKE YOU RICH. Things are so much better now, thank goodness! There were MANY low points! So, consider that. If you are 10 years old, you are old enough to realize that in 7 to 8 years, you will be graduating high school but the trajectory of your life can start to change if you want it to. If you are a slacker, please look at the most unhappy and unsuccessful person in your life and realize that you might be headed down that same path; I swear, you don't want that. Do you want to go to an HBCU? Which one? Say it every day. Get a sweatshirt from your favorite school. Find out what their qualifications are and start working on them now.

YOU WILL THANK YOURSELF LATER!

If you are already past that point and you bought this book because you were intrigued by the subtitle *For Girls 10-100*, YOU MUST KNOW THAT IT IS NOT TOO LATE FOR YOU EITHER. My best friend's mom went to college when we graduated high school. My mother was a cosmetologist for most of her young adult life, but became a published poet and started working for the school district in her late fifties; I am sure you have heard about the countless success stories connected to late bloomers. Instead of reading about it, make your own success story - I know that I am.

For me, in five years I will be married - happily married – with a family, and publishing more books, mentoring, writing new songs, creating films, and finding new and innovative ways to exploit my love of music and literature; my wild imagination will take care of me. I will have a successful and informative blog, will be super healthy, and will be a reliable resource for women in need.

Your turn. Write this down in your workbook or journal: *Where do I see myself in five years?* The only thing stopping you from being exactly where you want to be, outside of acts of God and nature, is your failure to plan and prepare. *Plan and prepare.* This question should be revisited every five years.

"The wise create proverbs for fools to learn, not to repeat."
~ African proverb

CHAPTER 2

Black & Be-You-Tiful

1. STAY HYDRATED!

Listen, anyone with dry skin is going to get ashy, but darker skin shows it more. Your skin is made to be silky, nourished, hydrated, and radiant; not cracked, dry, and thirsty. Chronic dry skin affects all races, but before running to the dermatologist or buying expensive cosmetic products, try a natural emollient. I say natural because the older I get, the more I hear that additives found in some skincare products are laced with carcinogens that cause cancer. My new rule of thumb is not to put anything on my body that I would not put on my heart. Heart? Yep, the epidermis, also known as SKIN is the largest external organ and the liver is the largest internal organ; in my mind, they work together. With that said, drink lots of water. Make it a habit to drink at least eight glasses a day and don't contrast the awesome benefits by filling your body with sugary drinks or alcohol. Our skin is thirsty for rich, emollient skin food and Shea, cocoa butter, and coconut oil seem to do the job just fine. Also, keep in mind that your entire body needs moisture. Our scalps should be oiled and exfoliated, as should our feet. I have learned those lessons the hard way…pun definitely intended.

2. GET THE APPROPRIATE AMOUNT OF SLEEP AND WAKE UP EARLY!

The early bird really does get the worm and if you have not already realized it, you will soon enough. According to www.BlackDoctor.org, our first lady Michelle Obama wakes up every morning at around 4:30am to work out. Awesome, right? This has always been a challenge for me since I am a songwriter and often record late into the night, but when my schedule permits I wake up earlier because it usually assures a better sleep cycle. Check out the sleep chart from www.SleepHealthJournal.org to see if you are getting the recommended amount of sleep every night. If you are not (like me), we must make this a priority because according to www.WedMd.com, "Black Americans are more likely than whites to get too little sleep and this disparity is greatest among people in professional occupations. A new study shows lack of sleep has been linked to an increased risk of health problems such as obesity, high blood pressure, diabetes, heart disease, and even death."

SCHOOL AGED CHILDREN, Ages 6-13

9 to 11 hours recommended, but 7-12 hours may be appropriate

TEENAGERS, Ages 14-17

8 to 10 hours recommended, but 7-11 hours may be appropriate

YOUNG ADULTS, Ages 18-25

7 to 9 hours recommended, but 6-10 hours may be appropriate

ADULTS, Ages 26-64

7 to 9 hours recommended, but 6-10 hours may be appropriate

OLDER ADULTS, Ages 65+

7 to 8 hours recommended, but 6-9 hours may be appropriate

3. YOU ARE NOT YOUR HAIR, BUT TAKE CARE OF IT AND EVERYTHING ELSE!

The hair on your head, your eyebrows, and lashes regenerate at a rate designed by nature, especially for you. However, once the follicles, scalp, or skin are damaged, it's very difficult to get it back to it's former glory. I totally understand the desire to keep up with the trends, which for whatever reason are sometimes the most damaging. My mom is a licensed cosmetologist so she almost always had an option for me when I came home with these crazy ideas like getting a perm or dying my hair jet black or platinum blonde, or shaving the sides, but some of you don't have that in-house wisdom. You can go wherever you want and buy whatever you need to change your look in an instant and to you, I say, think ahead. Instant gratification often ends badly. You will learn this in life. Also, setting trends instead of following the masses is probably what you really want to do deep down in your gut where it counts, so do that. I am not here to shame those that aren't down with the natural hair movement, but if you do get a perm, a weave, or even heavy braids, wait until it's age appropriate for you. Consider the side effects and be honest with yourself, especially when faced with the possibility of folliculitis. If you don't know what that it is, Google it now, look at the pictures, and study it in-depth before any treatment, process, or installation. Regardless of what you do, nothing should get in the way of you washing and conditioning your hair once a week and having your ends trimmed every six weeks. That coupled with vitamins and a close look at your lineage will help you to avoid so much anguish down the line. However, I MUST end on a happy note! We have the most beautiful and diverse hair in the universe. You can flip through the pages of Vogue and other mainstream magazines and see white women wearing cornrows, box braids, afros, crimps, and anything else that we have made popular…no shade, it's really true and it's my hope that you see that everyone wants what you have. The melanin in your skin has a radiant glow without the help of tanning beds or endless hours in the sun because you, my dear, are the black gold of the sun, so please shine brightly…it's your birthright!

4. YES, BLACK CAN CRACK!

Let's just jump right into this. We look good and are the leading ethnic group when it comes to "looking young" even at an advanced age thanks to melanin, but that doesn't mean that we are not susceptible to skin cancer and other ailments. According to www.SkinCancer.Org, "different ethnicities are at higher risk for particular skin malignancies: Latinos, Chinese, and Japanese. Asians tend to develop basal cell carcinoma (BCC), the most common skin cancer. But the second most common, squamous cell carcinoma (SCC), is more frequent among African Americans and Asian Indians." YEP, you read that right, we need sunscreen as much as the next ethnic group; just because melanin is resilient and has an extended shelf life, it is not indestructible. When you have a chance, visit http://blackdoctor.org/9595/best-sunscreens-for-blacks/2/ and choose the best sunscreen for you! In addition to sunscreen, be sure to MOISTURIZE! Commit to a skin regimen. The products have varied for me over the years and are really a personal choice, but every night before I go to bed and every morning when I wake up I wash, tone, and moisturize my face. I also exfoliate twice a week and apply a masque once weekly depending on what my concerns are. So many readers are at different stages in life, but the same advice that I have given my sister regarding taking care of her skin can be followed by a woman double her age.

Get creative and make your own skin scrubs. For instance, I mix 2 cups of raw (coarse) sugar, 1 cup of coarse salt, 1/2 cup of olive oil and 1/3 cup of melted coconut oil with a few drops of my favorite essential oil and slather it on my body! Afterward, I feel soft and beautiful! I have given them as gifts too.

Do not scratch and/or pop pimples. I know, random, right? You will thank me later! First of all, if your acne becomes unbearable like mine was for a short while when I was a teenager, make an appointment with a dermatologist instead of doing extractions on your own. I still have an indentation on my nose from when I had chicken pox, but my mom begged me not to scratch so much. I only scratched the one on the tip of my nose that I could not resist, but I have friends that scratched and popped and now they have dark spots to show for it.

DRINK LOTS OF WATER AND EAT A HEALTHY DIET! I know that I just mentioned this, but I can't express the importance of staying properly hydrated. There are tons of sugar and other horrible things in sports drinks, sodas, and even juice but water is not only safe, it's also required for the survival of ALL living things. Give your body, skin, and hair what it wants - more water. I am no scientist but I know that my skin and hair look so much better when I eat better. Www. BlackGirlLongHair.com has a list of eight foods that contribute to healthy skin and hair, and get this...chocolate is on the list! Please be sure to check out http://blackgirllonghair.com/2013/10/8-foods-for-healthy-hair-and-beautiful-skin/

5. WATCH YOUR MOUTH!

Both literally and metaphorically. I am absolutely against any form of censorship, but one of the things that hold us back both as a gender and as a people is this poisonous venom that shoots from our own tongues and cripples the next woman. I have met some strikingly beautiful black women, but when I hear them chipping away at the soul of another, it makes them hideously ugly to me. I don't need to spend much time on this because it's simple. You may see this come up several times because it's true in many cases - when you speak ill of someone else, it is only a reflection of your own insecurities. Also consider this, the same people that you gossip with will gossip about you, but you can't be responsible for them so watch the words that come out of your mouth and keep in mind that the things that you say about others should never be destructive. Obviously, no one is perfect; we all have shortcomings, but do not make a habit of talking trash. It minimizes your beauty.

Something else that minimizes beauty is premature tooth decay and gum disease. Yep, I said it; bad breath too. Sometimes you can brush all day and have perfect oral hygiene practices and still have issues with odor and decay. If that is the case, see your dentist. In fact, we should see the dentist twice a year for cleanings. Some dentists recommend cleaning only once a year, but that is up to you and your dentist. The beautiful thing is that in most circumstances, we have the power to keep our oral cavity healthy and clean by NOT SMOKING or chewing tobacco, by brushing twice a day, and flossing in between meals. Please do not underestimate the power of flossing. If the food stuck between your teeth isn't removed, it can harden, grow bacteria, and cause infection, ultimately resulting in tooth loss and periodontal disease, according to the CDC. But wait, that's not all! We must also address "gold fronts", "grillz" or whatever you want to call them. We see beautiful black celebrities like Beyonce, Rihanna, Teyana Taylor and Kelis rocking gold grills, but we don't consider the serious up-keep that is involved. According to www.MouthHealthy. Org, "If you wear a grill, you should be especially careful about brushing and flossing to prevent potential problems. Food and other debris may become trapped between the teeth and the grill allowing bacteria to collect and produce acids. The acids can cause tooth decay and harm gum tissue. Bacteria may also contribute to bad breath. There also is the potential for grills to irritate surrounding oral tissues and to wear the enamel away on the opposing teeth." If wearing a grill becomes a part of your daily routine, taking it off and cleaning daily should be a part of that routine as well. I know that some of you are reading this like "Yes, I can't wait to brush my teeth and floss", while others are more concerned with the cost of simply eating every day and oral care hasn't even crossed their minds. If that's you, please visit the Resource Center in the back of this book for tips on keeping your teeth squeaky clean while on a budget. In this case, "flossing" is cheap now and will cost loads more later... should you not floss at all.

6. THOUGHTS BECOME THINGS! THINK HIGHLY OF YOURSELF.

There is no one more beautiful than a black girl or woman with healthy self-esteem! I have a tattoo, a couple in fact, and the one that is most precious to me is on my forearm and it reads **"Believe. Become."** I could have put it in a much cooler place if it was for everyone else, but it's for me. Sometimes I need a reminder to keep my thoughts positive, but you don't have to have a tattoo to do that. Write something that resonates deeply within you in your journal or on your mirror and say it to yourself, especially when you don't believe. What resonates with you? Do you know that your value doesn't decrease based on someone's inability to see your worth? Do you know that beauty shines from the inside out and all of the make-up, sunscreen, and beauty remedies won't make a person with a negative view of themselves or an ugly heart more beautiful? Self-esteem can only be faked for so long because if you don't believe, no one else will. If you don't love yourself, no one else will. Obviously, this is all a process; you won't read this and suddenly have the best self-esteem ever, but changing your thoughts will do wonders for your life.

SIDE BAR: That subject line "Believe-Become" sparked a life changing email for me in 2011. It was a really low night and I was completely and utterly depressed. I had recently divorced someone that I was married to for twelve years and was dating someone exactly like him except younger, which was far from a good thing. I was mourning the loss of my time with Oprah Winfrey every day as she had recently aired her final show, but at the very end she gave out her email address and said that she would be responding to emails personally. I BELIEVED HER, but it wasn't until that dark moment that I decided to pour my heart out to this woman who had been in my life every day, beginning from the time I was a child. It was almost like we already knew each other and I had sooooooo much to tell her about the mess that my life had become. In the subject line I wrote "Believe. Become"; it was my new mantra derived by a friend of a friend who came to my birthday celebration, looked me square in the eye and said, "Think. Say. Be." That resonated more deeply with me than I had imagined. It was like hearing the gospel. If I think it, then verbalize it, I can become it? But only if I believe, will I become! That is how that mantra was born. I was later made aware that Buddha had the same thought thousands of years ago, but I do BELIEVE that I coined the specific phrase. Anyhoo, I wrote Oprah the longest email about things that I may never share, but it was so heavy that I actually felt lighter after pressing 'send'. I fell asleep with my computer beside me with an expectation that she would respond. A little while later, I rolled over and saw an email from Oprah@Oprah.com and almost passed out. False alarm. It was one of those blanket computer generated responses. I closed my eyes and fell into a light sleep; every noise sent my eyes flying open. Then I saw the second email. When I opened the email, I saw the words, "Taura, you win for the longest darn email I've ever seen." I have never been so happy to be jolted wide awake! She went on to write, "You BECOME, and are at this moment what you believe for sure. Your belief is an energy field that draws like energy unto you. To turn it around you have to change the field or vibration."

The rest of the letter is something that I will forever cherish and would only make public if 'Auntie O' says so. Yes, 'Auntie O'…she's the Auntie in my head, always has been. When I was a kid, I would come home from school and watch her show with my mom and her clients. Sometimes I would assist my mom by washing or blow drying hair and could hear my mom saying, "I'm going to turn Oprah off if you can't do your job", then I'd straighten up and fly right just so I could keep watching. In my young adult life, I took her with me when I moved to NYC after getting my first record deal. I remember people asking why I was so fixated on her, but I didn't care. Her words hit me in a place that I didn't know existed and I became better as a result of spending that hour with her every day. However, the day that she emailed me, I was not in a good place. There was one thing that she shared that changed the trajectory of my life and has landed me in the good space that I am in now. She said, "You believed you were not worthy of trust, respect, joy, love. And so you created an environment to reflect what you believed. See that and now create differently. Beginning right now. Pray. Ask for guidance. And be open to see it when it shows up. Prime example: me opening this email of the 131k that are in my inbox right now."

That was my "aha!" moment, with a one-two punch. The first thing that I realized is that my mantra was a one-way street. "Believe-Become" was this thought process where I thought that I would become only the best of my beliefs; but in that moment, I actually realized that I really had become the worse of my beliefs. I mean, I would say it like, "Good or bad, we all become what we believe", but my true belief didn't mirror that until it stared me in the face and I saw a reflection that was headed in the wrong direction. The other thing that struck me was that out of 131,000 emails from people just like me, she opened mine. I know that was a gift from God, because He knows how badly I needed to feel special at that low point in my life. She ended her letter with "Now my email is as long as yours. So I will stop. Got to pack for Africa. Going to see my girls.

Blessings,
Oprah Winfrey
Blessings to you, Taura"

I was humbled and forever changed. When the smile wore off and I began to dissect every word in that letter, the real work began. Soon after that life changing experience, Oprah named her third Life class, "You Become What You Believe".

Fast-forward to March 2017. I became a brand ambassador for O Magazine. Yes….I am pretty excited too. The group is called "O Mag Insiders". Starting this year, O Magazine is choosing fifty people to represent the brand, try new items, go to events, etc. and I am one them. If that's not enough, out those fifty, I was selected as one of twelve people to represent O Mag Insiders in the June 2017 issue. I am so looking forward to the future! *#StillBelieving #StillBecoming*

7. YOU ARE ONE OF A KIND!

It's true and when you start to believe that, you will then begin to see your true value. There is no one on this beautiful planet exactly like you. Be proud of that and be proud of you!

8. KNOW WHO YOU ARE!

This is pretty obvious, but as a child I didn't know this to be true. I thought that I was to do what my Mom said and that was it; trust me, that made me who I am and I am thankful for that, but knowing who you are early on will save you so much anguish in the future. If you know who you are, you are less likely to be bullied. Why? Because there is far less fear in the knowing and if you don't know who you are, someone else will try and tell you who you are or worse, who you are not. The scary thing about that is that often times people believe what they are told and go through life oblivious until they realize that they were not being authentic to themselves. You don't have to do that because starting now, from wherever you are, you are going to affirm who you are. Grab your journal and write it down. What do you believe? Not what your parents believe, but what do YOU believe? Who am I? As I mentioned previously, I am Christian and I believe in the way of Christ and the Ten Commandments, which may be a lot different than other Christians. I try my best not to be judgmental and I believe that Christ does in fact love EVERYONE! I am empathetic, compassionate, and a keeper of secrets. I have always wanted to be a writer and that's why I actually do this for a living. I am a fixer. I get things done. I am so much more, but I am also private enough not to share every interesting detail. If someone says that I can't write or cook, I know that something is clearly wrong with him or her, but that's how things have to be for you. You have to be so clear about who you are that other opinions in opposition to your truth are laughable. If you are a lesbian, you can't trap yourself in a closet and hope that nobody finds out. When things stay in the closet too long, they lose their color and get holes…don't lose your color, the world needs your vibrancy. If you are a plus sized girl like me, first know that your health is the most important thing but that is a personal journey for you and your doctor to decide, not some insecure bully or shallow boy that is dumping their poor home training onto your lap.

Lastly, I must address skin color and hair texture in this section even though it will likely pop up in other places in this book; it's just that important. If someone has something to say about you being too dark, too light, or points out that you have "nappy hair", don't let it knock you off of your path. The same people talking about your hair will be adding kinky Remy hair to their head as soon as it rolls around in the mainstream again. Black women went through hell in the '70s for wearing braids, were getting fired and asked to change their style, but when Bo Derek had her hair braided she was then credited with 'making braids famous"; suddenly they were acceptable. Years later, the same would happen when Kim Kardashian and Kylie Jenner started sporting cornrows. You don't need to wait for any validation. You are unique. You are NOT a carbon copy. KNOW WHO YOU ARE AND OWN IT! The same goes for anyone else who is lucky enough NOT to be normal. Normal is boring, anyway.

Being pro-black doesn't mean that you are anti anything! Shine your light not only on social issues, but socio-economics, gender equality, and the tons of other causes that require your support. Do not sit in the dark, suppressing your light. Your voice is the light. Your advocacy is your light. Your standing up for the rights of womankind is your light. Let it shine, let it shine, let it shine!

9. KEEP YOUR HEAD IN THE BOOKS!

One thing that I know for sure is that education is the key to escaping poverty and mediocrity. Sure, there are several exceptions to that rule since so many people have excelled or have led exceptional lives without a college education like myself, but I only responded to what was accessible to me. My mom was a single parent and keeping her stress free was and is one of the most important things in my life, so naturally when I heard everyone griping about how expensive college was, I knew that I was not going to go. All of my friends went to college, even my god sister Brely and our group member Mykah, and we were in a singing group together. I enrolled in a junior college but my mind was stuck on music and that was all that mattered, so I never finished…but I will because it's never too late to start again. However, I was inspired to write this book to keep you, the reader, whomever and wherever you are, from making the same mistakes that I have made. I am grateful to my mother for giving me book report assignments every summer, because I became an avid reader long after the reports were due. With that said, college may or may not be in your future because it is a choice, but either way keep reading; it is fundamental. There is nothing worse than a woman who is beautiful but can't offer an intellectual viewpoint to a conversation. (Whisper: But I strongly suggest that you go to college).

10. DO WHAT YOU LOVE AND IT WILL LOVE YOU BACK!

When I initially started writing this, I thought that I would certainly DEMAND that every black girl reading this would make a pledge to further her education, but life is about choices and there are so many people that went to college and became successful doing things that they hate. Loving what you do is essential. Not everybody wants the fancy cars and house on a hill. Some are happy with traveling the world and being of service to those in need. Bre'ly owns a company called *Water Walkers, Worldwide* and she urges people to get out of the boat and walk on water. What a stunning visual, because you MUST have faith in order to believe that you can do the impossible, and guess what? YOU CAN! "Get out of the boat and do what you love and you will never work a day in your life," she says. When I was working on a particular film, there were several songs involved. Sounds easy enough, right? I write songs, they pay me, then I go home and chill. NOPE! Film studios have a team of people with different ideas and opinions for your creation...and so begins the rewrites. My primary writing partner for the greater part of my career and brother from another mother is Raphael Saadiq. He marveled at how excited I was to make the changes. I was never upset. In fact, I was challenged and the song almost always got better with every revision. I attribute this to loving what I do. If I would have become an accountant, this story would be very different, but music loves me back because I loved it first. What do you love? Write it down, because in years to come you may find that you will love it just the same.

When there is no enemy within, the enemy outside cannot hurt you. ~African proverb

CHAPTER 3

You Are The Power!

The next generation has the key to turn EVERYTHING around, but only if we are around to fight, tell our stories, stand up for our rights, and stop being the key group impacted by far too many unfavorable statistics. I am sure that you have heard the term "you have the power", but have you ever considered that you ARE the power? Each and every one of you is an energy source that can spark monumental change. As a people, we are counting on you to turn things around.

1. CHECK YOURSELF TO PROTECT YOURSELF!

Breast cancer statistics are downright scary. White women are more likely to get it, but black women are more likely to die from it. How is that? In my mind, that means that there is a lack of preventative measures taken on our behalf, not to mention a lack of resources. However, if we start to change the stigma attached to check-ups, mammograms, and visiting the doctor, change will come. Generations to come, meaning YOU, have the complete power to change this statistic. According to the CDC (November 2012), "approximately 40,000 women die of breast cancer each year in the United States, but BLACK WOMEN ARE MORE LIKELY TO DIE OF BREAST CANCER THAN WHITE WOMEN." It goes on to say that black women have the highest death rate of all racial and ethnic groups and are 40% more likely to die of breast cancer than white women. The reasons for this difference result from many factors, including having more aggressive cancers and fewer social and economic resources. To improve this disparity, black women need more timely follow-ups and improved access to high-quality treatment. Also, only 69% of black women start treatment within 30 days of being diagnosed compared to 83% of white women. So, I am hoping that you, yeah you, the one holding this book, know that you are now responsible. You have life saving information for yourself and your loved ones. Clearly there are not as many resources out there for us, but we can't continue to let that be the reason why we are winning this race to death's door. I have compiled a few that you can refer to in the Resource Center, but should you be faced with this monster, I urge you to dig. If you do not have a computer, go to the library. If you do not have Internet, go to a coffee shop or hell, jump on the neighbors WiFi if you can. This is a "By All Means Necessary" type of situation, and time is clearly of the essence. What will you do? Have you had a mammogram? What about your mother, grandmother, sister, cousin, auntie, or other female family member? Do you think that you are too young to organize a community screening event? **I DARE YOU TO!**

2. BE POSITIVE THAT YOU ARE NEGATIVE!

We are leading in HIV statistics as well. I recently read some startling statistics about Atlanta being the HIV capital of the United States, but when you look at the map at www.aidsvu.org/map/, it is apparent that this is a wide spread issue that is infesting our communities everywhere. Looking at the highly affected areas, it is obvious that EVERYONE IS AT RISK and that includes you if you are having unprotected sex, sharing needles, or participating in other risky behavior including sharing cocaine straws or being so inebriated that you don't remember or care about the consequences of your behavior. I need to debunk one theory here, as well. HIV studies have made monumental strides and the life expectancy has likely quadrupled since the 1980's, back when it was a definite death sentence. Now, you can lead a full and extremely healthy life with the help of drugs, but DON'T GET IT

TWISTED, *AIDS STILL KILLS*! If you are sexually active and do not know your HIV status, you are doing yourself a disservice. If you are not yet sexually active, stay that way until you are in a fiercely committed partnership or married. In a perfect world, a.k.a., my world (HA!), that's how it should be but I know better. My mom told me to keep my panties up and my dress down and I did that for the most part, the other part would have been much easier had I listened completely. Let's stop there for a moment. If not already, most of you are sexually active. Some of you will be wild and irresponsible while others are the opposite, avoiding multiple partners. However, both of you will be at risk. No matter how faithful, devoted, pretty, sexy, or even smart you are, you are not exempt from being exposed to someone who has had multiple sexual partners. The best way to avoid this is abstinence of course, but I live in the real world so I know that many of you will not choose that route. If you don't, I am really hoping that you choose to protect yourself. Nothing feels as good as a negative HIV test. When you consider having sex for the first time or even the next time, read up on HIV and other sexually transmitted diseases before you lay your life down.

3. ALWAYS LISTEN TO YOUR HEART!

According to *The Black Women's Health Imperative*, www.bwhi.org, "Black women suffer rates of heart disease that are twice as high as those among white women. Some of the factors that contribute to this disparity include higher rates of overweight and obese women, higher rates of elevated cholesterol levels and high blood pressure, and a limited awareness of our elevated risks. In addition to having high heart disease rates, black women die from heart disease more often than all other Americans." My beloved aunt, Vanessa Dean Williams, died of heart disease. She had a heart transplant and lived for about five years before passing away and I miss her dearly. I'm certain that you know someone who is impacted by heart disease as well and if you don't, with statistics like this, you certainly will. I am personally struggling every day with my weight. I am considered obese and I feel the heaviness of that weight affecting me as I get older so unfortunately I am the perfect person to speak about this. My sister Brely and I were in a music group together, and we thought we were equivalent to farm pigs. We obsessed over every photo of ourselves thinking, "Wow, look how fat we are!" Girls, don't will obesity into your lives. Don't wish fat on yourselves. We were perfectly fine in our little singing group, Emage, and far from overweight, but didn't I tell you that good or bad, you become what you believe? I am proof of that.

I am also proof that guarding your personal space is paramount and essential to a healthy life. Our hearts house our emotions too, so when someone is telling you on the daily that you are fat, ugly, and worthless, you start to believe it. I was repeatedly told how unattractive I was by someone not worth mentioning. At first, I didn't believe him but I had no choice but to be impacted by what was being said to me daily. In both scenarios, I was perfectly fine but in time I became what I believed. This speaks to both the physical and emotional effects that could very well lead to heart disease. When I look back at our video, I was perfectly fine. I was hit by a car when I was 18 months old, so I have never been able to wear a half top like Brely and Mykah, but I was fine as wine, as were they, and our weight issues were just figments of our imagination. I think that it started with the record label telling us that we needed to lose weight, but do you know that if we knew who we were already, nobody would have been able to tell us anything at all? Now many years later, we are, in fact, overweight but very well aware that it's time to make a very serious change; this time for the right reason. In 2009, with the help of Dr. Dre & his wife Nicole, who are complete fitness gods, I lost 76 pounds. They hired a trainer, Linda R. Lee (who, by the way, epitomizes *awesome*) to train me. I put my mind into it and lost so much weight, but honestly it was for the wrong reasons so it didn't stay off. I did it to save my marriage, not my life, and when things were not right I returned to old behavior. My point in sharing all of this is to be as transparent as possible so that you do not make the same mistakes that I did. If you are not losing weight for the betterment of yourself, there is a strong likelihood that you will gain it back. Now my heart is at risk but the silver lining is that this time, I am doing it for Taura. I also don't have room for negative people in my life. Sometimes I would feel so terrible about myself that I could feel my heart rate dropping like I was on roller coaster, and that is never good for the heart. Smoking is also bad for the heart...I used to do that too. I can't even believe that I would waste so much of this precious breath on something that could have killed me. The upside to all of this is that often, things can be done to undo the damage that we have inflicted on ourselves. According to BWHI, "Many of the heart disease risk factors can be controlled by making small improvements that can lead to large benefits. For example, losing only 10 to 20 pounds can help lower your heart disease risk. Other steps to reducing heart disease risk include:

- Learn the risk factors and the symptoms of heart disease and if you have them, see your doctor.

- Don't smoke.

- Eat well-balanced meals that are low in fat and cholesterol and include several daily servings of fruits and vegetables.

- Engage in at least 30 minutes of a moderate-intensity activity such as brisk walking or another activity that you enjoy such as dancing at least five days a week. If you need to, divide the period into shorter time frames of at least 10 minutes each.

- Know your numbers. Have your blood pressure and cholesterol levels checked regularly to ensure that they are in a healthy range.

- Keep your blood pressure, blood sugar, and cholesterol under control."

Always protect your heart, ladies. Physically and emotionally.

OKAY! READY FOR SOME GOOD NEWS? WHEW, I KNOW THAT I AM!

4. THINK TWICE BEFORE YOU START A NEW LIFE.

According to www.AmericanProgress.org, "Birth rates for teenage African American women from ages 15 to 19 decreased by 7% from 2011 to 2012." But get this, the Department of Health and Human Services reported a 9% decline from 2013 to 2014! This is great news because it's evidence that we are starting to get a better understanding of how life works. Getting pregnant at 15 years old means that you are stopping your life's progress to start another; raising a child isn't easy. I'm not a mother as you know, but I have witnessed several family members and people in general have children at a very young age, and for the most part they have struggled to make ends meet. It's also like a domino effect. The mother of the pregnant teen or someone in the family usually has to supplement and care for the child because the father isn't even a man yet and most often can't be there for the mother of the child or the child itself during that period. Most often, the teen mother misses out on huge life moments like high school graduation, prom, and college. According to www.NCSL.com. "Only 40% of teen mothers finish high school and fewer than 2% finish college by age 30." The obvious problem with that is that if you don't have a high school diploma and in some cases, a college degree, breaking the cycle is a huge challenge. Now, I am completely aware that there are exceptions to this rule. In fact, my first cousin Joya got pregnant and married when she was 19 years old.

Her dad was furious because he had high hopes for his daughter, but she proved him and everyone else that doubted her wrong. When it was all said and done, she got her Master's, a PHD, and raised four impeccable children; one is headed to Yale this fall on a full scholarship. If that isn't enough to spin your wheels, she and her husband are still married and they are two of my favorite people in the world, but I REPEAT...this is not the norm! First off, she graduated high school with honors and was a student at UC Berkeley when she got pregnant. When she had her first beautiful daughter, Zaria, and the bills started pouring in, she didn't give up. She transferred to a less expensive school and she and her husband took turns going to college; they both graduated. They also had a built-in support system with both Billy (her husband) and her own parents helping to take care of the children. It was a unique situation. I shared that story for the girl who is pregnant and reading this now. You have to try a hundred times harder than you ever have before. It will be hard but you can do it, with or without your child's father. Please visit the Resource Center for valuable resources designed specifically for you and your child. If you have already had a child and you are a teen, don't give up on yourself. Be brave enough to break the cycle. Don't sit there wallowing in self-pity or count yourself out. You have got to get up and fight. Lastly, if you are NOT pregnant, make a vow to yourself to wait it out. Be the best YOU that you can be before becoming a mother. See the world, graduate college, and wait until you are properly aligned with your soul mate before being responsible for another soul.

5. CONTINUE TO EDUCATE AND ELEVATE!

According to www.ClutchMagazine.com, "Despite the misconceptions and stereotypes about African American women, we are making great strides in education. In addition to half of all black women ages 18-24 pursuing higher degrees, black women are beating out ALL other groups, no matter the race or gender, when it comes to overall college enrollment. According to the data, 9.7% of black women are enrolled in college. Asian women are second with 8.7% working toward degrees, followed by Asian men at 8.4%, white women at 7.1%, black men at 7.0%, Hispanic women at 6.6%, white men at 6.1%, and Hispanic men at 5.9%." THIS IS AMAZING NEWS! Now all we have to do is keep that fire burning. Unfortunately, reports that parallel this story show that we are still being underpaid and that, my sistahs, is where *you* come in! DEMAND TO BE PAID EQUALLY! Imagine if 9.7% of black women demanded equality? Imagine if 100% of the 50% of women that are ages 18-24 and pursuing higher education hired highly qualified black women to become executives at their companies, doctors at their hospitals, and educators at their institutions? We are standing together at the college level and we have the numbers to prove it. Now it's time to implement this system in the workplace.

6. KNOW OUR HISTORY!

When I was in school, we learned about American and World History all year long and focused on Black History only in February. That clearly isn't enough, so the only option is to educate you further. The more that we know about our past, the less likely we are to face similar atrocities in the future. The more that we know about the injustices imposed on our ancestors, the more likely we are to vote. Www. BlackPast.org is a phenomenal resource for anyone who would like to know more about our resilient people. In the first ten minutes that I perused this site, I learned that the first black female mayor of a major US city was Sharon Pratt Dixon, mayor of Washington, DC in 1991. I nearly spit out my coffee. 1991? I graduated high school in 1991, thinking all was well with the world. In retrospect it's shocking, but it's just as shocking that nearly thirty years later, unarmed young black men and women are being killed by the police. When I look at the list of "firsts" on Black Past, the same juxtaposed feeling that I had when Halle Berry was the first black woman to win for Best Actress in 2001 rises up in me again. That feels like yesterday…we have such a long way to go and the only way to get there is for us to go as a unit. Do yourself a favor and spend lots of time on this website. It's filled with gems.

7. TALK ABOUT IT AND BE ABOUT IT.

The only way that the narrative will change is if we are standing for and speaking our truth. What do you fight for? What do you want to fight for? What can you fight for? In this day and age, you must have an answer for one of those three questions. I am passionate about equality for women of color but my fight is just starting, so don't feel bad if you are late to the game, just get off of the bench and play! We were silent for too long. We were SILENCED for too long, now it's time to speak up.

8. HEAL YOUR MENTAL ILLS.

According to www.BlackWomensHealth.com, "Black people account for approximately 25% of the mental health needs in this country though they only make up 11- 12% of the national population. To make matters worse, only 2% of the nation's psychologists are black. The rates of mental health problems are higher than average for black women because of psychological factors that result directly from their experience as black Americans. These experiences include racism, cultural alienation, violence and sexual exploitation." Only 2% of the nation's psychologists are black? How can they help us if they don't know us? I hope that this inspires some of you young ladies to get your degrees in psychology so that our people see a familiar face and hear a familiar voice when they finally gather the strength to go and see about their mental health. I touched on this twice in this book because it's a serious issue that plagues us black women and out of everyone living through the turmoil, I only know one young lady who openly speaks about being bi-polar while the rest of us are "perfectly fine" on the outside, but are clinically depressed or battling mental illness within. Www.BlackDoctor.com suggests contacting a medical professional if you or a loved one experience five or more of the symptoms below for a period of two weeks:

- A persistent sad, anxious or "empty" mood, or excessive crying
- Reduced appetite and weight loss or increased appetite and weight gain
- Persistent physical symptoms that do not respond to treatment, such as headaches, digestive disorders, and chronic pain
- Irritability, restlessness
- Decreased energy, fatigue, feeling "slowed down"
- Feelings of guilt, worthlessness, helplessness, hopelessness, pessimism
- Sleeping too much or too little, early-morning waking
- Loss of interest or pleasure in activities, including sex
- Difficulty concentrating, remembering, or making decisions
- Thoughts of death or suicide, or suicide attempts

9. FIGHT TO STAY ALIVE!

Karyn Washington was the founder of the website "For Brown Girls" as well as the founder of the project #DarkSkinRedLip. She committed suicide at 22 years old.

Titi Branch was a natural hair pioneer and the co-owner of a widely successful, multi-million dollar company, Miss Jessie's Hair Products. She committed suicide at 45-years old.

Tovanna Holton was a 15-year-old high school student who committed suicide when bullies shared a nude video of her on Snap Chat.

These are three tragic examples of women whose pain was so deep that they took their own lives. Karyn had recently lost her mother and didn't know how to cope with the depression that comes along with losing a parent. According to several media sources, it's alleged that Titi was at odds with a controlling boyfriend, and Tovanna was bullied by her classmates. I am positive that at least one of these circumstances have occurred in your life and if it hasn't, it likely will. It's my deepest hope that if you even have an inkling of a whisper of suicide in your soul that you speak with someone before it becomes so loud that pure silence seems to be the only answer. Can I tell you that SILENCE is never the answer? You are here for a purpose and keeping you here, happy and whole, is one of my main goals in life. When I was a kid, I thought of suicide as a way to escape the bullies. My refuge was often the nurse's office and after being harassed by a group of girls, I went to the nurse's office and cried myself into the worse headache ever. There were Tylenol or some sort of pain relievers on the counter and while the nurse wasn't looking, I took more than I should have. I believe the number was six. When she came back in, she asked me if I took the pills and I said "Yes", then "No, no, no" when she picked up the phone to call my mom. Minutes later, my mom was there since we literally lived up the street. She had tears in her eyes when she asked me why I took so many pills. I wasn't honest. I told her that I had a headache, which I did, but honestly, I just wanted to sleep. I was so tired of those girls verbally and physically assaulting me every chance that they got. When I woke the next morning, I was so happy because no one knew the number of pills that I took except me, so I wasn't sure if I had taken too many. Soon after that, I learned to fight back. I was no longer a sitting duck who would only shield myself when they came for me. Instead, I defended myself and it's my hope that all of you do the same. Defend yourself against yourself if you need to and by that I mean talk to someone that you trust. Go and visit a medical professional. Talk to your parent or guardian about your suicidal thoughts because thoughts really do become reality. Www.SPRC.org states that "Although black suicide rates are lower than the overall U.S. rates, suicide affects black youth at a much higher rate than black adults. Suicide is the third leading cause of death among blacks ages 15-24. Since the black community in the United States is disproportionately young, the number of deaths among youth may have a particularly strong impact on the black community. Black Americans die by suicide a full decade earlier than white Americans. The average age of black suicide decedents is 32, and that of white decedents is 44." If you are having thoughts of suicide, please contact the National Suicide Prevention Lifeline, now. 1-800-273-8255.

Sure, love will hurt your heart emotionally. Break ups hurt HARDCORE, but that's NOT the kind of hurt that I am talking about. Regardless of how bad it feels, you WILL heal from even the most tumultuous break up, but there's something that isn't cancer, HIV or some other nasty disease that could potentially kill you. There isn't a way to ease into this, so I will dive right in. If your significant other is punching, kicking, pushing, choking, slapping, smothering, burning, pricking, stomping, or cutting you, you are in a domestic crisis and need to LEAVE NOW! It isn't love, so there's no need to stay for the sake of it. He will do it again, so there is no need to believe otherwise. According to http://www.doj.state.or.us/victims/pdf/women_of_color_network_facts_domestic_violence_2006.pdf , "African American females experience intimate partner violence at a rate 35% higher than that of white females, and about 2.5 times the rate of women of other races. However, they are less likely than white women to use social services, battered women's programs, or go to the hospital because of domestic violence." 35% is a low number in my estimation. Those numbers represent the women that had the guts to report it, but what about the ones who have not? I know this far too well because I was in two terribly abusive relationships…yet another reason that I felt compelled to write this book. One of the "guys" (let's call him that because even at ten years my senior, he was NOT a man; he was a grown boy who was terribly insecure and dependent on others) had poison festering in his tongue long before he ever laid a hand on me. It started with verbal abuse. For so many years, I believed everything that he said and even gained weight because I heard him call me a fat B-Word so many times that I started to believe it, and eventually lost the desire to be present in my own life. If that is happening to you, please do not give him the chance to prove himself. Just go. LEAVE. Run! There are so many stand up men out there in this big world and you do not need one that is defecating on your self-esteem. Furthermore, you don't NEED one at all. You could live a happy and productive life by yourself and welcome a significant other if and when you darn well please. But back to this "guy". His behavior took a turn for the worse soon after we moved in together and I found myself fighting for my life on several occasions. Just like the women depicted in the statistic above, I didn't tell. I was raised in Oakland far before the gentrification project that is making Oakland "cool" again. People used to gasp when I said I was from Oakland and now they smile fondly, and although I have ALWAYS loved it, it is a very different place than it was when I was growing up; you didn't snitch. You just didn't do it. It's such a bizarre rule that only fares well for street thugs and people that lead a life of crime and those that are afraid of them. Well, I was afraid of him. He always told me these scary stories about his family, but in hindsight I now know that he was bating me. He knew that he was a woman beater and he knew that he had to change me because I came in strong; I was confident, successful, and unstoppable. The very first time I met him, I was disgusted. He came to a friend's funeral to meet me. I said "Hello" and "Goodbye" within thirty seconds of meeting him, but he didn't give up. We ended up working in the same space a year or so later and he was terribly obnoxious, arrogant, loud, and ignorant. I was so turned off and should have followed my first mind, which said "Stay away from him." A few weeks after that, two mutual friends reached out to me regarding working with him on a project and I declined after the first attempt, but conceded when I got the second call. I was in a vulnerable place in life and did something that I am not proud of. After months of working together, I began to grow fond of him and we started seeing each other. I had just ended a relationship and he was still in one. I didn't know her well, but I knew myself and the girl code well enough to know that it was wrong, so I broke it off with him until he broke it off with her. Then he and I seemed to go 200 miles an hour and I knew that it felt wrong, but I kept going until he smashed me into a brick wall. Not literally, but that was the impact my decision felt like. Our relationship progressed and soon after we took a huge step, the physical abuse began and didn't stop until I finally got the guts to pack up and go. Over time we had amassed all of these "things", but the things didn't matter. I just wanted my life. A year earlier, he chased me down the hallway in a drunken rage with the gun that was given to us as protection for me when he was away. His best friend saved my life by tackling him to the ground. I ran out of the house and got into my car without a second to spare. He ran up to the car and all of a sudden, glass shattered everywhere. I thought that I was dead. I thought that he shot through the driver's side window, but he had punched it. Yes, he had that much anger and that much force to obliterate tempered glass. Can you believe I forgave him after that? I know some of you are like "Dummy!", but this is a notice for you all to be certain about who you counsel with. I spoke with someone, not either of my parents but someone whom I trusted, who told me to fast, pray, and take it to God. The "guy" then started going to church again and suggested that we move to another house because the one we were in was "evil". Ha, can you believe the next house was "evil" too? Why? Because HE was in both of them and he started to lose it even more so, if that's possible, in the second house. One of his good friends who was staying there with us told me that I should leave because he often talked about killing me. I knew it to be true because he always told me that he wanted to beat my head in with a hammer, and not just any hammer - a big mallet type hammer that he actually bought for very specific reasons and it was truly the grace of God that protected me. He went out of town and I packed my dogs, clothing, pots, pans, spices (because I love to cook), and my guitar and I left. I left the new leather sofa, the new flat screen TV, and everything else that meant nothing to me and I left. Throughout the course of my time with him, he had been with numerous women, "friends" of mine included, so I wanted to make him hurt the same. There was this young guy that would stay with us from time to time. FYI, people were always staying with us because we had a recording studio in our house and quite honestly that's what the "guy" wanted. Anyway, this other guy was right there saying "I can't believe he treats you like this…I would never…" To make an even wilder and more gruesome story shorter, I kissed him while I was still with the "guy" and to be honest, I felt vindicated for a few hours. Then guilt set in. I knew that leaving was the best thing. A year earlier, after the near-death experience with the gun, I KNEW that I was going to leave, but I was so afraid of what would happen to me. Music was all I had ever done but my royalties were so up and down. I thought, "How will I take care of myself?" I literally called everyone that I knew that was well aware that I was qualified to work at a label or publishing company and NO ONE called me back except for the most unlikely source of all - Paris Hilton. I wrote and vocal produced for her debut self-titled album and we became friends, but even more so after she called me back in the middle of the night while she was traveling and told me not to cry because I could start as her personal assistant. To this day, I am perpetually thankful to Paris for changing my life. I still had that job when I left "the guy". I was casually talking to "Guy 2" when I left, but he preyed on me like the monster that he was and likely still is. He knew EXACTLY what to say, because unbeknownst to me, he was the devil with a handsome face. Casual soon turned exclusive and I left Brely's house, where I was staying after leaving "the guy", and moved into my apartment. Guy 2 helped me move in and never left. It was like he was Dr. Jekyll and Mr. Hyde. His eyes would literally change before my eyes and then he would get very violent, then cry like a baby. I was so embarrassed to tell anyone that I had slipped into the same black evil water again and that I was drowning, so I kept it to myself for as long as I could. Then one day, I called one of my best friends, my brother Raphael, and I told him that I needed to talk to him. I went to his studio and told him what I had been living through almost daily. I asked him not to tell my parents and he said he wouldn't but he then had a change of heart. He called me one day and said "If something happens to you and I am the only one that knows this, I could never live with myself so I need you to tell your mother or your father and the ONLY way that I will be satisfied that they know is when one of them tells me so." I hung up the phone and all that I could think about was facing the realization that everyone would know that I was abused, AGAIN. My former manager, someone that I really respected, said that I must like being beaten, which anyone with sense and compassion knows that not to be true, but I knew that that would be the general consensus among the chatter. I had no choice. I had to tell my mother or father. I told them both as soon as Guy 2 left to visit his family for the weekend, which came right on time since he was very violent with me the night before he left. My next-door neighbor went to the manager to tell him that she heard him being violent before but became increasingly concerned once she was certain that what she was hearing was extreme domestic violence. At the time, I was working as an assistant for Sean Puffy Combs and I swear to you, every day after work this guy accused me of sleeping with security, the chef, female co-workers, or Puff himself and then he would become violent. When I write this, I feel like I am a girl in some movie and now I'm in the audience screaming, "RUN, RUN!". It really was that simple, but because I did not allow myself time to heal and get help from a psychologist after leaving the first loser, I accepted, tolerated, and even attracted the same thing. When I finally told my parents, my father told me to tell the guy that he was on his way to stay with me, and to change my locks; there would be consequences to pay if he showed up. This is all so hard to share, but I couldn't back down. I am writing this to help YOU, the young girl or seasoned woman who may face similar unfortunate circumstances. I cannot express enough how important it is for you to *run*. Chances are not meant to be given to abusers. There will be people that dispute that, but I don't care. I feel that a person can walk the straight and narrow only for so long and then they will have a psychotic break that may end your life. But I didn't believe this at the time of my very toxic revolving door type relationship with this guy. When he went up north, what he was really doing was reuniting with his child's mother and beating her as well, but I would find that out later; he told me that he was in counseling, that he wanted to speak out against domestic violence at schools and he seemed to be totally different. I fell for it, like an idiot. He came to Los Angeles some months later after passing what he called 'intensive abuse and anger management counseling' with flying colors. We planned to take it slow, and he could not know where I lived. So, he had a show in LA and I even sang background vocals for him. Raphael came, I think partly because he wanted to make sure I was okay. I WAS NOT. Later that night, I stayed with him at his hotel and he attacked me. For the next week or so, I was literally his hostage. I knew he was crazy at this point and I knew that I had to get away but I felt trapped, embarrassed, and scared out of my mind. I couldn't even tell my mom that she was absolutely right when she said I should NEVER be around this guy again because he would kill me. How could I tell her that he had been there since his show, monitoring every call and going with me everywhere? He kept me away from my friends, just like he had done before.

I believe his show was on a Thursday. That Sunday, he was crying, apologetic, and thought we should go to church. We went to Pastor Toure' Robert's "One Church" that was located in North Hollywood at the time. When we were in the parking lot, he snapped, saying that I made us late. He slapped me, then put a smile on his face and held my hand as we walked through the doors of the church, which was packed, so packed that we were lead to the front row; I have NEVER sat in the front row of any church, but it was meant to be because the Word was for me. The pastor talked about being good and how it would come back to you. He called several people by name, including me. He said, "God knows your heart, Taura." I knew him for years, but he had never called my name in church. By the way, he was calling names from all over the church, not just the front row. This set the guy OFF. When we drove home, I knew that it was going to be tragic. I cried like I was a little girl, knowing that I was going to get a whooping. He surrounded me like a tornado when we got to MY apartment, but he learned to keep quiet since my neighbor couldn't stand him. That day seemed to have gone on forever as he held me in the kitchen at knife point, promising to kill me for sleeping with the pastor. I pleaded with him, letting him know that the pastors then wife, Lori, was a friend of mine. He wasn't buying it. At the end of the day, I had a black eye and it felt as if I was holding a seashell up to my ear. At the time, I was helping Raphael out at his studio and he was prepping for the tour, but I couldn't go to work on Monday. I looked like I had been beaten up, because I had been. I could justify not going that Monday, but Tuesday was a must since he was leaving on Wednesday. That Tuesday morning, I got a work-related call. I was working as an A&R for Mathew Knowles' Music

World and one of our clients called me to discuss an impending conference call. He said something like, "When the call starts, I have some things that I will address but please do not take it personally because it's not aimed at you…I like you." I had the call on speakerphone as he demanded, and as soon as he heard that, his horns flared. When I hung up the phone, he asked "Why did he say that he liked you?" Before I could answer, he jumped on me, choking me to the point where I knew that would be the day that I died. In that moment, I knew that I HAD to fight back. I used the pinch of strength that I had left, raised my knees to my chest and kicked and pushed at the same time, sending him literally flying across the room. In that moment, my phone rang. It was Raphael asking what time I was coming to the studio. That saved my life, because all this guy wanted was a shot at fame and working with Raphael was one of his goals in life. I got dressed and put a bunch of make-up on to cover the bruises. I also had a cold and every time that I blew my nose, I could hear the air seeping through my ear. (Deep sigh. This has been the hardest thing to write. It took me three weeks of erasing and rewriting…pausing)

He reminded me that since Raphael and his band were leaving the next day, I would have nowhere to run and that he would kill me. I believed him. When I got to the studio, Raphael instantly knew something was wrong so he mentioned it to our mutual good sister-friend, Monet Owens. She came into the office and when I had a moment away from the guy, I told her that something was terribly wrong but I was so afraid to tell her that I went to the bathroom and wrote it down on a napkin. This way, if he knocked on the door, I would just flush it down the toilet. However, he didn't so I was able to write it all down in tears, with mascara running down my face. I gave her the letter that ended with, "He is going to kill me today, please call the police." When the police came, they told me that he had a warrant for the same charge in his hometown. They had a female officer come to make a report on my body. Monet stood in the bathroom with me as I stripped down to nothing in front of a mirror in tears. My body looked like a corpse. It was purple, blue, battered and bruised everywhere. I had a bruise that the officer described as the size of a watermelon that wrapped around my side to my stomach into my back. When I removed the make-up from my face, I had a black eye and busted vessels in my eyes from the choking. I also had his hand prints around my neck. It was gruesome, and all possible because I believed that he would change. It was a horrible situation that I would eventually heal from but it took counseling, prayer, and time. For once in my life, I stood on my own two feet with nobody to lean on and realized that I had been holding myself up all along.

Guess who's holding you up? Right, you! Of course, God designed the plan but He gave us GPS, cars, legs, wheelchairs, planes, and this huge thing called FREE WILL. Yes, a woman carried you in their womb and fed you, but when she gave birth to you, your time - as you know it, began. She or someone else walked with you and showed you about this thing called life, either through a beautiful or challenging view, but one thing is certain; you are, or will eventually be, on your own and when you are, choose you. Choose happiness. Choose honesty. Choose freedom. Choose life. Choose to scream it from the mountaintops and send the fool to jail that evah-evah puts his hands on you. Choose to be strategic on how you get yourself back into a safe place surrounded by people who love you, even if the "people" is that one person named 'you'. Choose to force yourself to understand the things that float above your head, especially this chapter, because YOU REALLY ARE THE POWER. You are the power that will change every negative statistic that plagues us today. You are the power that will enlighten those that are in the deepest and darkest space. You are the power that will cause legislators to change unfair, racially divided and gender biased laws, and you are most definitely the power that will knock the socks off of anyone that punches, kicks, chokes, slaps, smothers, burns, pricks, cuts, shoots, stabs, sexually assaults, defiles, or assaults you in any way. In order to be a part of the fight, you need to be here. Please choose to be here. If he thinks that his freedom is in danger, he will only be more violent. Move quietly and only discuss with the authorities and people that you really trust. Most importantly, when you get away from him, never look back. If he knows your schedule, change your routine and make other changes like changing your locks or your address. Call the police station and find out what's available to you locally. There is a way out and no, this is not love and yes, he will do it again.

10. SEEK WISE COUNSEL.

Most of the trouble that I got into was a direct result of my ignorance, or because I sought advice from one of my friends who in all honesty was just as much in the dark as I was. You have the power NOT to do that. If you haven't seen the person overcome an obstacle that you are facing, it may be wise to wait and seek the advice of someone who has been through similar things. When I think back at some of the advice given to me by some of the people that I love dearly, I laugh hysterically because often it was a clear case of the blind leading the blind, but you, you with this book in your hand, have so many resources available to you, so use them. You have the power to overcome and dispel stereotypes and myths, and honestly, whatever you put your mind to. Always consider the source before diving head first into someone else's plan. Another thing to consider is your own intuition, water it with wisdom, and LISTEN. Often times, the answers are there if we just hush long enough to hear clearly.

When there is no enemy within, the enemy outside cannot hurt you. ~African Proverb

CHAPTER 4

Back Pocket Wisdom

"Look both ways before crossing the street" is the one of the first solid pieces of advice that I remember following. It's pretty obvious that if I don't look both ways before crossing the street, a car may hit me because I cannot rely on the other car to look out for me. That's pretty simple, but other pieces of advice aren't as clear, like "Don't play with fire." You won't really take that to heart until you have firsthand knowledge that fire is actually hot and can burn you. Some need a teaspoon of fire to know that it actually burns while others require a gallon, but the ending consensus is that fire is in fact, hot. The next ten "things that you should know" will never change. They are common but too essential to assume that you already know them and while certain things change with the times, these will never change so keep them close to you…I call it 'back pocket wisdom'. It's not in your hand for all to see, it's deep in your back pocket where no one can see but you know that it's there.

1. LOOK BOTH WAYS BEFORE CROSSING.

That goes for streets and people! This will mean different things to each of you, so I will let it resonate in whatever way it lands. Just remember that you look both ways before crossing streets to avoid getting hit by a vehicle, but in general you must understand that this is also a metaphor for life. Looking both ways for me means to consider where I have been and where I would like to be before agreeing to anything. For you it might mean seeing both perspectives in a disagreement or considering words of wisdom from your parent or guardian, along with your own wisdom, before making a decision.

2. WASH YOUR HANDS FREQUENTLY, ESPECIALLY BEFORE EATING.

The "pretty" reason for washing your hands is that you protect yourself and others from the spread of bacteria, disease, and infection but the "dirty" version is a lot more urgent. According to the CDC, "Hand washing with soap could protect about 1 out of every 3 children who get sick with diseases, as well as diarrhea and pneumonia, the top two killers of children around the world." I still see adults not washing their hands and shake my head. If you have one in your family, call them out! Your safety depends on it.

3. BE CONFIDENT.

Sounds simple enough, because it is. There is something deep inside of your soul that you are confident about. For me, there are a few things. I KNOW that I am a good person. I KNOW that I am a great friend. I KNOW that I am a BOMB cook! I KNOW that I am great with WORDS. What do you KNOW about you? The process of getting to the KNOWING is simple. First, search within yourself for what you KNOW for sure about yourself and build on that. When I was a kid, a cousin of mine found my notepad and couldn't believe that I had written such an amazing song at around 9 years old and in that very moment, a seed was planted inside of me that would later blossom into a full career. Sometimes you will have to plant your own seeds and that's okay. Battling with weight issues made it difficult for me to be confident about my appearance, so I had to plant those seeds myself. I KNOW that I have nice eyes, hair, and a great personal sense of style, but I also KNOW that those things will eventually fade away so the kind of confidence that matters most comes from the inside out. Quick, before you forget - write down five things that you KNOW about yourself in your journal!

4. KEEP YOUR TAXES, YOUR CREDIT, AND YOUR GOOD NAME IN GOOD STANDING.

If you are in grade or middle school you are probably thinking, "What are you talking about?" But it's so important and I am honestly not certain if you learn the importance of taxes and credit in the classroom. I know that I didn't. As a result, when I got my first big check from songwriting, I spent it. Years later, the IRS made it very clear to me that they are serious about getting their share; yes, *their* share. That percentage varies based on various variables including your income bracket, but one thing is for sure, if you are earning income or plan to, you should also make sure that you have a solid plan in place to pay both your state and federal taxes. If you want to learn more about your state taxes, visit your state's official website or give them a ring for more info; you might get lucky and actually live in a state that does not have state taxes. If you want to learn more about federal taxes, please visit the following link for information that you will keep with you for as long as you are on this earth: https://apps.irs.gov/app/understandingTaxes/student/hows.jsp

Your credit score is super important to your financial well being and being careful with it is what you MUST do if you want to make it work for you. I went to junior college briefly following high school and the first person that asked me if I wanted to sign up for a credit card in exchange for a t-shirt got a 'yes' from me. The problem was, I did not have a job to pay the bill and just like that, my credit started to go downhill. As a result, getting a new car and even an apartment was a struggle until I started to get it together. If you want to buy a house, you need a fair credit score. Same with a car and several other necessities like college, but condition your mind right now to KNOW that credit cards can also be dangerous if used in the wrong way. You could find yourself in terrible debt if you open up cards to support your shopping habits, so try your best not to be THAT girl. You know, the girl with all of the latest handbags and clothing who bums rides from her friends. Instead, be the girl that's so comfortable in her skin that she doesn't need "things" to make her feel more valuable. Be the girl that can buy a duplex in college, renting one of the units to students at a rate that pays for her own place. Be the girl that can buy her own car or get approved for her own apartment while everyone else is reliant on their parents or boyfriends. By the way, BE THE GIRL THAT NEVER NEEDS HER BOYFRIEND TO DO ANYTHING FOR HER. Be the "I've Got This" kind of girl. Deal? DEAL!

5. FIGHT FOR GENDER EQUALITY.

According to www.NationalPartnership.org, "On average, women in the United States who work full time year 'round are paid 79 cents for every dollar paid to men. For African American women, the gap is larger. African American women are paid, on average, just 60 cents for every dollar paid to white, non-Hispanic men. When women lose income, their economic security and that of their families is diminished." This is a problem that we are counting on you to solve in the next generation as we provide you with the building blocks, today. GRAB YOUR WORKBOOK.

Let's call this exercise "WHEN I GROW UP". The fun thing about this exercise is that EVERYONE can do it.

The question that you are going to answer is *"When I start my own _____company, I plan to have _____employees."*

The second blank space is for the number of employees that you plan to have, but don't worry if you don't plan on starting your own company. In that case, please put the number of people that you would like to manage in your department or serve in any given community.

For instance, if you plan to be an A&R executive, list how many people you want to oversee. Don't go crazy…remember that thoughts become things. If you can't figure out what to put in the blank, maybe you want to be something like a doctor, nurse, lawyer, teacher, mountain climber. That's perfectly fine but the question is a little different. *"When I become a _____, I plan to reach _____people."*

This is great, because ten years from now or even more, you can look back at your answers and see if you are on the right track.

Okay, now that you have answered the first question, I'd like for you to make a statement and be honest; a vow or pledge, if you will.

Of the _____ people that I said I would oversee, employ or reach, I hereby pinky swear in the name of gender equality to make sure that _____ are women.

The second blank represents an amount, like the number of or a percentage, even if it's one or 1%, just be honest. You may revisit this sometime later, after learning how much harder we have to climb as women, especially black women, and you will then have a better understanding. Until then, don't just take my word.

Visit the Research Center for studies on gender equality and why it's essential for our growth.

6. CHALLENGE YOURSELF.

The more that I read, the better I write. It's just a fact, but while I was an avid reader as a child, sometimes it's super challenging for me to read as an adult because life pulls me in so many different directions. The easy thing for me to do is not to read, but the reward comes after I face the challenge and my writing benefits from it. The same goes for fitness for me. The easy thing is to eat pizza and tacos whenever I want, but when I challenge myself to eat healthy, I feel and look better and my body operates at an optimal level. Challenge yourself in small ways, like not participating in gossip or drinking more water, or big ways like signing up for a marathon or volunteering at the homeless shelter on the weekend when you'd rather be at the beach. The rewards often can't be measured, but meeting the challenge always makes one feel accomplished. You can keep up with your challenges by writing them in your journal.

7. REMEMBER, WHAT GOES AROUND COMES AROUND.

I am sure that you have heard this before. If not, you will and believe me when I tell you that it's true. If you are kind to others, kindness will be extended to you but if you are not so kind, someone will be not so kind to you too. Sometimes what some call "karma" or "reaping what you sow" shows up quickly while it can take years in other cases, but one thing is certain, it *will* come. With that in mind, treating others the way that you want to be treated should be the goal in friendships, relationships, parent/child relationships and any other "ship". But beware, this doesn't mean that you give a friend an ice cream cone and should expect one in return. "Give" because it's out of the kindness of your heart, not because you are expecting something in return.

8. ALWAYS LISTEN TO YOUR GUT.

You are a spiritual being carefully crafted and encased in this shell of flesh called a body, but your spirit and your flesh will often be at odds...spoiler alert, the spirit always wins. Call it your soul, intuition, God's voice, the universe, the ancestors, an angel, or whatever you want as long as you listen. The spirit will tell you when a person doesn't mean well for you, when the body says, "Well, he IS cute". The spirit will tell you to come to a complete stop at the red light and the body will tell you to partially stop because you're running late or pull over and get out anyway, and that could lead to a dangerous result. The spirit will tell you to stay away from somebody that may get you in trouble and get this, sometimes the heart and body come together against the spirit to try and convince you to do what the spirit has already warned you about. I know this may sound confusing, but it'll make sense one day. In the meantime, discuss this in detail with someone that you love and trust like your parent, siblings, or close friends. Grab your journal and write down what the spirit says to you and better yet, write down a series of events where you listened or did not listen to your intuition. This exercise will help you to have a reference point because we tend to get convenient amnesia when it comes to matters of the heart. Having a reference point to remind yourself of what your inner voice sounds like could be useful to you in the future.

9. REALIZE THE IMPORTANCE OF HONESTY AND INTEGRITY.

I read a quote, *"Integrity is choosing your thoughts and actions based on values rather than personal gain"*, so BOOM…do that and you will sleep well at night.

Integrity isn't like a light that turns on and off depending on the time of day or who's around; it should always be with you and over time if you exercise it, it will become stronger and brighter. See, we learn things that aren't good, be it at home, school or even from music, TV shows, movies, social media or the internet, but there is a little compass inside of us that keeps us aligned.

Another quote from an unknown author reads, *"There's something wrong with your character if opportunity controls your loyalty."* To put that into perspective, abandoning a really good friend to hang out with the cool kids because it will make you more popular is not integrity. Having integrity will keep you honest and in fact they go hand and hand. You cannot have integrity and be a liar, cheater, or thief but don't beat yourself up if you make a mistake. We *all* make mistakes…and life is a journey filled with both sunshine and rain. Sometimes you will slip in that rain, but all you have to do is get up and try again.

Telling the truth is hard sometimes too. When I was a kid, I was an only child with a super wild imagination. As a result, I created this sub-reality by making up these ridiculous stories, like Prince was my boyfriend and Michael Jackson too, at one point. I can laugh about it now because I realized my mistakes and got my integrity in check; you can do the same thing. Don't ever think that you are a bad person because you have made mistakes, been dishonest, or acted out of character. Just don't stay on the dark side too long…it's harder to find the light when darkness blankets you!

10. LOVE AND RESPECT YOURSELF AND OTHERS.

If you have been reciting the mirror mantras, then you already know a thing or two about self love, but it's really so important that I needed to mention it twice, especially since loving yourself is a process.

As humans, we are always changing and evolving, so we have to learn to love ourselves at various stages of life. If everyone could start loving themselves as toddlers, that would be awesome but sometimes we need a little reminder or push, so please allow this book to be that for you.

Respect and love go hand in hand and work better together like peanut butter and jelly. If you respect and love yourself, you will demand that of others at every corner you turn in life.

Just don't be afraid to start where you are. You are worthy of the best that life has to offer and once you start believing that, your entire view will become clearer. Respecting and loving others presents a different challenge, but do it anyway. I respect and value my Jewish, Muslim, and Buddhist sisters even though we have obvious differences because we are all taking part in this human experience at the same time and fighting about who is wrong or right goes against my core values. When it's written down it seems so serious and official, but honestly, it's easy to do. Hatred and disrespect require too much energy.

THIS ESPECIALLY INCLUDES YOUR ELDERS. Respect and have the utmost reverence for your elders. I completely and utterly love and respect my parents and I am sure that they are well aware of this. I do not say or do certain things in front of them and that does not mean that I am being fake, it's just that I respect their boundaries and where they come from. Sometimes my music choices are far too ratchet to play in front of them but the playlists change when my girls and I are in the car.

This may help someone. Screaming at your mother or father because they weren't present when you were a child will not change their attendance record to "HERE". You have to decide if you are going to allow them to be in your life and this goes for anyone. If you have forgiven someone, walk in that forgiveness. Relieving terrible moments of yesterday is only going to convolute tomorrow. Choose to forgive, let go and move on, even if you need help. Choosing those three actions will prove to be so valuable in the future. Even with all of the terrible things that I have endured, I have still forgiven them. We can't fly when we have emotional baggage tied to our hearts. LET IT GO!

When it comes to your peers, using force of any kind, be it physical, verbal, sexual or emotional is NEVER okay.

* Punching the smaller girl to show her how powerful you are is disrespectful and could get you suspended.

* Rolling your eyes at the new girl at school or work, because deep down you really think that her hair, skin or clothes is prettier than yours, is whack. Make a vow now to compliment the things that you are fond of because you never know how that small compliment could turn her day around.

* Calling someone an ugly black b-word on social media is not okay, just as sharing the latest picture of some celebrity that you don't even know that shows her in a compromising position, even if it's just a meme, really isn't okay.

We have become this society of digital gangsters that throw up signs and throw serious blows from the comfort of home, and it's time out for that. It's a conscious choice because it's so much easier to react to everything that we feel, but the harder course is almost ALWAYS the most rewarding.

"Until the lion learns how to write, every story will glorify the hunter." ~African proverb

CHAPTER 5

THE NOT SO "PRIVATE" PART

Say "vagina." Say "vulva." Yell "VAGINA!" Yell "VULVA!" Sound it out, slowly: "Vaaa-giii-naaa", "vulll-vaaa."

"Vagina" is NOT A DIRTY WORD and neither is "vulva". The vagina is nothing to be embarrassed of and it's definitely not your "private"part. It is a life source that needs to be handled with care and openly discussed. I am not opposed to nicknames, but as with anything or anyone else, you have to become extremely familiar before being comfortable enough to assign pseudonyms. So ladies, meet your vulva and vagina. Not your lady part, p*ssy, tuna, box, c*nt, vajajay, cooter, muff, snatch, clam, taco, kitty, cat, downstairs, down there, girlie part, girlie bit, hoo-hah, "you know what" or anything else. It's your vulva (the outside) and your vagina (the inside) and the sooner that you get to know them, the better.

1. GET TO KNOW YOUR VULVA FIRST.

Say "vagina." Say "vulva." Yell "VAGINA!" Yell "VULVA!" Sound it out, slowly: *Vaaa-giii-naaa, vulll-vaaa.* "Vagina" is NOT A DIRTY WORD and neither is "vulva". The vagina is nothing to be embarrassed of and it's definitely not your "private" part. It is a life source that needs to be handled with care and openly discussed. I am not opposed to nicknames, but as with anything or anyone else, you have to become extremely familiar before being comfortable enough to assign pseudonyms. So ladies, meet your vulva and vagina. Not your lady part, p*ssy, tuna, box, c*nt, vajajay, cooter, muff, snatch, clam, taco, kitty, cat, downstairs, down there, girlie part, girlie bit, hoo-hah, "you know what" or anything else. It's your vulva (the outside) and your vagina (the inside) and the sooner that you get to know them, the better.

- **Mons pubis (1) -** The pubic area or fatty area directly above the anatomical split.

- **Prepuce of clitoris (2) –** Small crease-like area at the very top.

- **Clitoris (3) -** The small button-like gland underneath (2). According to Wiki, this is the human females' most sensitive and erogenous zone and generally the primary anatomical source of human female sexual pleasure.

- **Urethral opening (4) –** This is the opening to the urethra. According to Wiki, the urethra is a tube that connects the bladder to the urinary meatus (a passage or opening leading to the interior of the body) for the removal of fluids from the body. In other words, your urine passes through that urethral opening.

- **Labia minora (5) –** This is the inner labia, inner lips, vaginal lips or nyphae, according to Wiki.com.

- **Labia majora (6) –** If you guessed "outer" labia, then you are right. The labia majora are what some refer to as the lips and what most mistake for the vagina. It's the vertical fatty area that encases your vulva and vaginal opening.

- **Vaginal entrance (7) –** It is the opening and larger hole south of the urethral opening. It leads to your uterus, which leads to your Fallopian tubes, which lead to your ovaries. This very path begins the cycle of life. If you are old enough, you know what that means. If you are just getting a full understanding of what that means, **GRAB YOUR WORKBOOK AND WRITE DOWN HOW YOUR**

PARENT OR GUARDIAN EXPLAINED "THE CYCLE OF LIFE". PLEASE ALSO SHARE YOUR EARLIEST MEMORY OF HOW YOUR WERE TOLD CHILDREN ARE MADE. Check back and/or share with friends for a good laugh.

- **Anus (8) -** The anus is the opening that leads to your colon, rectum and intestines. It the passage that directs your feces out of your body.

- **Perineum (9) -** This is the area between the vulva and the anus but the perineum stretches to allow newborn human heads to emerge through vaginas. The perineum offers support to both the anus and vagina in both the male and female, so maybe this book will give it a better name.

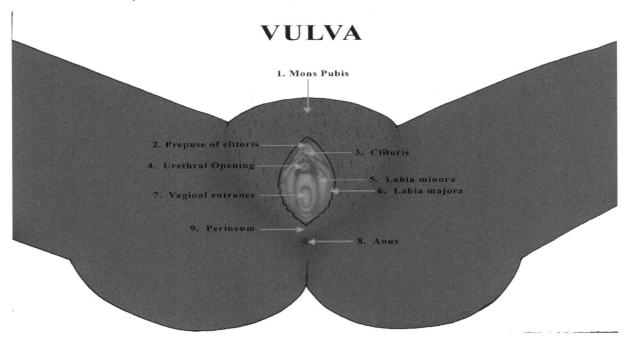

VULVA

1. Mons Pubis
2. Prepuse of clitoris
3. Clitoris
4. Urethral Opening
5. Labia minora
6. Labia majora
7. Vaginal entrance
9. Perineum
8. Anus

SIDE BAR: *According to Wiki, the Antenatal Perineum massage or birth canal widening massage has been used for many centuries by both Chukchi Eskimos in Siberia and by African tribal people. https://en.wikipedia.org/wiki/Perineal_massage*

2. YOUR VAGINA AND VULVA NEED YOUR HELP!

First off, they need you to know the difference between the two of them. When you read a very cool trendy blog about vaginal care and wonder why all of a sudden you are known as the smelly girl in ____(insert wherever you are), don't blame yourself. Blame everyone that didn't tell you that your vagina does not need soap. It's an internal organ. Does your heart need to be scrubbed down with tons of fragrances and cleansers that you slather on your body? Of course not. Does your vulva? Say no to anything artificial, but there is a chance that it may need a little help freshening up. We'll talk more about that later, there is so much to learn. According to http://grammarist.com/usage/vagina-vulva/, the vagina is the passage leading from the opening of the vulva to the cervix of the uterus. Most sources recommend that girls should see a gynecologist between the ages of 13-15 but things are so different now. We are living in a sexually charged, lightning-fast paced society that may call for a revision to that timeline, but before a doctor's visit is scheduled to either comply with that timeline, or because it becomes necessary, a female should first be familiar with her own vulva and vagina.

I can't recommend a specific age or even an age range because it's solely based on the individual, but I do know that the longer the vulva and vagina is shrouded in secrecy, shunned, frowned upon or whispered about, the more intrigued the young lady will become, and she will more likely explore, so facing it with openness is the ONLY option. The first on a list provided by WebMd.com entitled *Your Vagina: 7*

Things Every Owner Should Know is "Know What Your Girl Parts Look Like". The site recommends using a hand-held mirror to check things out and I can't think of a better way, but having a reference point is important too. Be sure to note any questions that you may have and save them for your visit with your gynecologist. If you are already beyond that point, it's good to note that exploring your vulva every now and again isn't a bad idea either. In fact, it's important to note that good vaginal health begins with you, no matter how old or young you are. The doctor will often follow your lead based on your findings during self-exploration, so write it down and don't be afraid to ask any questions. Your body. Your rules.

1. THERE IS A SHORT LIST OF WHO SHOULD BE ALLOWED TO TOUCH YOUR VULVA/VAGINA.

The subtitle of this book is *For Girls 10-100*, so if you are on the left end of that spectrum you are likely taking your own showers and baths by now. If you aren't and your parent or guardian is still bathing you, or you have a handicap that does not allow you to wash your own vagina, then you are the exception to this rule.

TELL YOUR PARENT OR GUARDIAN, SCHOOL COUNSELOR, OR THE AUTHORITIES IF ANYONE ATTEMPTS TO, OR SUCCEEDS AT, TOUCHING OR GROPING YOUR VULVA, VAGINA, BUTTOCKS, OR BREASTS, KISSES OR HUGS YOU INAPPROPRIATELY OR INSTRUCTS YOU TO TOUCH THEIR PENIS OR VAGINA.

Also, be sure to tell your parent/guardian/trusted adult or authorities if someone is attempting to make contact with you that you have met online. Even though this book was written for girls 10 years and older, this rule applies to those that can talk. For further clarification, we need to spread the word within our families that it is NEVER APPROPRATE FOR ANYONE TO TOUCH A CHILD SEDUCTIVELY. Little girls and boys both need to know that someone will take their claims seriously and that they will be safe if they "tell on someone". Again, a child being touched seductively by any adult is NEVER OKAY. Also, there should be ZERO SECRETS BETWEEN YOU AND ANOTHER ADULT THAT YOUR PARENT OR GUARDIAN DOES NOT KNOW ABOUT!

If you feel uncomfortable, it's probably because it's wrong, so please tell somebody. This also means that teenagers shouldn't be touching you either. When I was a kid, maybe 10 years old, my neighbor tried kissing and groping me repeatedly. He was almost 18 years old, and all of the girls in the neighborhood thought that I was crazy for pushing him away, but I knew better. My mom always told me to tell her if anyone touched me, but I was embarrassed to tell my mom so I told my cousin instead. She was close in age to him and I'm not sure how that conversation went, but he barely even looked my way after her visit with him. It's important that you have someone like that in your life.

4. PERIODS END SENTENCES, NOT LIVES.

I was pretty sheltered as a child. When I discussed life-changing events like the start of the menstrual cycle with friends, they were expecting it, or at least had conversations about this with their parents. But when mine came, I was completely oblivious. My mom would ask me things like, "Have you started your period yet?" And I would scoff "No", but I really didn't know what she was talking about. So naturally when I started, I thought that I was literally dying. I remember wearing off-white painter pants with splashes of neon paint on them (give me a break, it was the '80s) when a girl in my class said "Eeew, she started her period." I knew that it must have been me since my mom kept asking. I went to the bathroom with one of the loud mouths in class following closely behind. She helped me position myself in the mirror where I could see the carnage in full effect. At first I thought that it was paint splatter until she said, "No, you started your period. Go and look in your panties." My stomach completely swallowed my heart when I realized that she was right and before the day was over, I was sitting on top of folded brown paper napkins from the girl's restroom as my classmates filled me in on what they knew, which wasn't much more than I had already known at that point. I went home, folded up some much more comfortable toilet paper into a huge wad and threw my panties into the trash. My mom didn't find out until the next month when I was sent home with debilitating cramps and an even more embarrassing bloodstain. She hugged me and told me that it wasn't the end of the world and now it was more important than ever for me to keep my panties up and my dress down. I didn't realize then that she was most fearful of me getting pregnant at a young age like so many girls in the neighborhood and that's a valid concern, but if you are just starting your period, congratulations to you on your womanhood! This is a not a death sentence, but a life sentence. According to www.BeingAGirl.com, "Every month or so, the uterus lining gets thicker to prepare for a fertilized egg if the woman becomes pregnant. If the egg doesn't get fertilized, that lining is released from the body as blood through the vagina. This monthly process is called menstruation, or a period." So, yes, starting your period is an indication that more than likely you can conceive a child, but it is also ushering in puberty and significant changes in you. During this time, your breasts will grow and you will start to develop pubic hair, curves, and key defining attributes that separate girls from women. Embrace it, but do not chase it. You have the rest of forever to be an adult woman, but this transitional phase only comes once. ENJOY IT! There is so much information out there about menstruation and puberty and I encourage you to immerse yourself it in, but here are a few things to consider right at your fingertips.

1. Prior to the start of your first period, you should go shopping for tampons or maxi pads.

2. FYI! When your breasts start to form and you start growing armpit/pubic hair, your period may soon follow.

3. Girls generally start their periods at 12 or 13 years old but it really depends on the person. You could get it earlier than 12 or later than 13 in some cases.

4. According to the Huffington Post, "After studying 17,000 girls, researchers concluded that among white girls, the average age of breast budding was 9.96, while it was 8.87 for African-American girls. Until then, the generally accepted age was 11 or so. (For unknown reasons, studies consistently have found that, on average, African-American girls develop earlier than white girls.)

5. When you get your first period, make note of the start and end of it. This is generally a good practice that should not end. Note that it may up to two years for your period to become regular. Consult with your gynecologist for more info.

6. According to www.TeenHealthSource.com, "the average length between periods is 28 days, however you may have your period more frequently than this. Most women have a menstrual cycle length somewhere between 21-35 days."

7. Periods usually last between 3-7 days.

8. When you start your period, changing your pad or tampon every 3-4 hours is ideal. Sometimes your flow will be heavier and require more changes, but even if it's light, try and change it every 3-4 hours to avoid toxic buildup that could result in toxic shock syndrome. It's also documented that bacteria starts to form within that time frame as well, so change your tampon or pad even when it isn't completely saturated with blood. With puberty, your sweat glands and body hair will change and most of you won't be able to play outside without needing deodorant. Please choose a paraben and aluminum free deodorant as both ingredients have been linked to breast cancer. Check the resource center for options.

9. DISCHARGE BEFORE AND AFTER YOUR PERIOD IS NORMAL. For more information, please visit this link http://blackdoctor.org/452874/decoding-your-vaginal-discharge/

5. YOU ARE FEELING DIFFERENT BECAUSE YOU ARE!

According to www.Teens.WedMd.com, "Puberty usually starts between the ages of 8 and 13 and lasts a few years. It may start earlier in girls who are overweight, or later in girls who are very athletic or thin. If you are 12 and haven't started developing breasts or are 15 and haven't gotten your period, your doctor will probably want to examine you to make sure everything's OK. During puberty, your body releases hormones that stimulate your ovaries to start producing the female hormone estrogen. Gradually, a girl's body starts changing into a woman's body. But these surging hormones can also make your mood go up and down and sometimes it may seem as if your body is out of control." Don't let anyone tell you that you have an attitude problem or that you are an angry black girl or woman. Do not feed into the stigma associated with being black: confrontational and ghetto. We are complex beings with millions of inner working parts that can change at any minute. I have even heard that black people in general are more emotional and all that I can tell you to debunk every one of those theories is to never generalize. You are you. You are an individual and there is no one else in this world like you. You may approach puberty with ease while your friend may have a hard time with it. Lend her a hand, don't make fun of her or call her mean, impossible or that "B" word that you are not supposed to be saying in the first place. But I digress (smacks lips and clears throat), the WebMD article also explains why most girls are taller than boys. "Most girls experience growth spurts early in puberty, while boys have them later in puberty, that's why many girls are taller than boys in middle school." Translation? You are not Godzilla. If you are taller than the boys at your school, it's just nature taking its course. If you are gaining weight, it's also nature taking its course. When I tell you that you will wish for that "fat body" in twenty years, you may not believe me, but it's true. I cried about not being as small as the other girls, but now I wish that I could fit the Jordache jeans with the blue and white striped sweater that I wore when a friend and I dressed alike at Frick Junior High School in Oakland. See how many details I remember all of these years later? I really want that "fat" back, hahahaa! One last thing, ladies. Breasts develop in puberty as well. Web MD says, "Along with gaining curvier hips, your breasts grow during puberty. Inside them, a network of milk ducts develop. This is your body's way of preparing you to nurse a baby when you're older." The operative word being "older", but I digress yet again. Some of you may have small breasts or huge ones, either way they are yours and you should never feel ashamed of them or feel compelled to change anything about them. For the longest time, one of my breasts was much larger than the other, but my mom assured me that no one could see it as much as I could. If you are experiencing the same thing, please know that it is not as bad as you think.

6. THE VULVA AND VAGINA OWNER'S MANUAL

Let's start here! Your vagina is not supposed to stink. Don't believe me? I'll say it again! *Your vagina is not supposed to stink and neither should your vulva.* Sure, it will have an odor, especially following exercise or if it's a hot day, but generally speaking, it should only have a slight odor. If it smells "fishy", there is likely a problem, especially if the odor is accompanied by discharge, itching, burning or pain, but before panicking, the first thing that you should check is your hygiene practices. Visiting http://www.faqs.org/health/Healthy-Living-V1/Personal-Care-and-Hygiene-Genital-care-for-females.html is like informational Disneyland. Explore the site for as many helpful hacks as you desire, but back to our lady business. HYGIENE IS SUPREME!

- **WASHING AND DAILY CARE**

The vagina cleans itself, but your vulva will need a hand from you. The crevices are where odor-causing bacteria may hide, so be sure to wash the area thoroughly with warm water but soap may or may not work for you and as a result, a great number of gynecologists recommend that we nix soap all together and wash with water only, but I am learning that that's a personal choice. A great deal of gynecologists recommend washing with soap only while others recommend gentle, fragrance free soaps like baby soap or Aveeno. Whatever you do, do it every day and possibly twice a day if you have

had an active day or if it's particularly hot outside. Be sure to include the perineum and anus area when washing your vulva.

I am in agreement with medical professionals who don't recommend douching. The vagina cleans itself and douching could disrupt happy flora and change your PH balance.

SIDE BAR: Www.VeryWell.com explains those vaginal floras are the bacteria that live inside the vagina. The normal vaginal flora is dominated by various lactobacillus species, which help to keep the vagina healthy by producing lactic acid, hydrogen peroxide, and other substances that inhibit the growth of yeast and other unwanted organisms. According to http://www.intimina.com/blog/vaginal-ph-importance/, "PH is a scale of acidity and alkalinity. The measurements range from 0 to 14: a pH lower than 7 is acidic and a pH higher than 7 is considered alkaline. A healthy vaginal pH is between 3.8 and 4.5 – so the vagina is healthiest when it has an acidic pH level."

- **EATING FOR VAGINAL HEALTH**

Www.EveryDayHealth.com notes that eliminating foods that contain simple sugars (including some fruits), white flour and rice, and anything fermented with yeast such as alcoholic beverages and bread may cure or prevent yeast infections.

Maintaining a healthy diet will help you to also maintain your feminine PH balance. According to www.simpleorganiclife.org/vaginal-health-1796284936.html, yogurt has good bacteria cultures for a healthy vagina while garlic has antimicrobial and anti-fungal properties. Garlic may not be on your menu, but dark chocolate is good for your vagina too. It's high in flavonoids, which is an antioxidant. Drinking water is what they call a "no brainer" as being hydrated is good for your whole body. Nuts and seeds are also great for vaginal health because they are high in vitamin E, which prevents dryness, but fall more in love with pumpkin seeds and almonds which are both high in zinc and combat itching as well as regulate the menstrual cycle. For more detailed information, please visit the link above.

- **ODOR CAUSES, PREVENTION AND GOOD HYGIENE.**

Your vagina will have a slight, musky, earthy scent but it is NOT SUPPOSED TO STINK!!!!!! If it does, it's usually related to a problem.

If you have a fishy odor, coupled with itching, and/or burning and a thin grayish-white or yellow discharge, chances are you have bacterial vaginosis, an infection that affects nearly a third of women. According to www.medic8.com/healthguide/vaginosis/what-is-bacterial-vaginosis.html, "Bacterial vaginosis is not a sexually transmitted infection (STI) or sexually transmitted disease (STD), because the bacterial imbalance that occurs can be the result of causes not related to sexual contact that upset the natural pH balance and bacterial levels in the vagina and/or urethra. Virgins can get bacterial vaginosis, but, having vaginal intercourse, having multiple sexual partners, and also having an STI or STD can increase the likelihood of bacterial imbalance and bacterial vaginosis."

If your vagina smells like baked bread or beer and you are starring in your own personal itch festival, and it's coupled with a clumpy, cottage cheese like discharge and a swollen vulva, you more than likely have a yeast infection (Monilia or Candida Albicans). There are more than a few over the counter treatments for yeast infections, but seeing your doctor for a proper diagnosis, especially if it's the first time, is a good idea.

If your vagina smells like bleach or ammonia, there is a chance that your PH balance may be off, or if your vagina is carrying the scent of semen, ultimately you should see a doctor as it could mean a sexually transmitted disease or something more serious.

Obviously, being physically active can cause the vulva to sweat and become musty, just like your underarms. Let's park there for a second, especially since we are talking about hygiene!

According to www.Cancer.org, "Aluminum-based compounds are the active ingredients in antiperspirants. They block the sweat glands to keep sweat from getting to the skin's surface. Some research has suggested that these aluminum compounds may be absorbed by the skin and cause changes in estrogen receptors of breast cells. Because estrogen can promote the growth of both cancer and non-cancer breast cells, some scientists have suggested that using the aluminum-based compounds in antiperspirants may be a risk factor for the development of breast cancer." With that said, I have recently switched to deodorant, and apparently, I am super late to the party. My friend Candace stopped using antiperspirant a decade ago simply based on the premise that she does not want to "force quit" any of her naturally occurring bodily functions, so she uses aluminum-free deodorant in place of the antiperspirant. This wasn't a foolproof transition for me, simply because I am so used to feeling completely dry under my arms. Finding the right deodorant took a little time and now I have the perfect fit. You should find one too. When you do, be sure to apply it according to the directions on the container.

Okay, back to my point regarding smells associated with physical activity. The solution is simple. Shower after you have been baking in the hot sun. Shower after you have played a game of basketball, soccer, or cheerleading. Shower. Shower. Shower.

Wiping from the front to the back after urinating protects your vagina from potential cross contamination from the anus that could result in a urinary tract infection. It makes perfect sense, doesn't it? I remember being told this when I was a kid and had the hardest grasping the concept of wiping front to back but it got better with time for me, just like it will for you.

Also, try your best to wear cotton underwear. I know that they are not always the prettiest, so wear them according to how you feel. If you feel irritated, itchy, or just like something isn't right, ditch the thongs and fancy underpants and trade them in for good ol' cotton.

- **MENSTRUAL CARE and OVERALL HYGIENE**

Yes, you can take a bath while on your period. It can be visually overwhelming if you have a heavy flow, but there is no danger posed to you should you decide to take a bath while menstruating. Additionally, don't forget to change your pad or tampon every 4-6 hours.

PRODUCTS AND INGREDIENTS TO AVOID:

- **Dyes/Man-Made Fragrances/Perfumes**

- **Parabens** – They are synthetic preservatives that mimic the effects of estrogen and is known to cause breast cancer. Avoid it all costs.

- **Talcum powder** – Women have used it for years to keep themselves and babies dry, but it has been directly linked to ovarian cancer. Avoid it at all costs.

- **Phenoxyethanol** – It is used in both perfumes and insect repellent, so no questions here, right? It's also a known carcinogen. Avoid it all costs.

For more detailed information, please visit, https://www.collective-evolution.com/2012/04/10/you-have-the-right-to-know-17-chemicals-to-avoid-in-cosmetic-and-personal-care-products/

THINKING OF HAVING SEX? YOU NEED TO TALK WITH SOMEONE THAT YOU TRUST FIRST. If you don't have anyone to talk to, please check out the Resource Center for a few choices and ideas.

7. WHEN TO SEE A DOCTOR.

- **Discharge**

The first time you have abnormal discharge, you should see your gynecologist, period. Do not try and diagnose yourself, especially if you are sexually active. In fact, if you are sexually active and your partner is not using condoms, you could have a sexually transmitted disease or a sexually transmitted infection, both of which can cause infertility and even cancer if overlooked. Normal discharge is typically sticky, clear, translucent, white and odorless. That's good discharge. Bad discharge usually smells, is lumpy, yellow or slightly green, which brings me to the next thing that you should know about.

- **Sexually Transmitted Diseases and Infections**

You can sit in sexual education class all day, but if you don't make a commitment to value yourself, none of the information matters. Being a good judge of character is one of the delights in life. It will save you time, trouble, pain, heartache, and even your life. It's easily applicable to countless situations, but sex is what we are discussing here so let's jump right into it. Having unprotected sex is not the smartest idea. I don't recommend it until you are married and even then you have to exercise choosing someone of good character for a mate, because a marriage license and a diamond ring does not guarantee fidelity and if it doesn't have a guarantee then consider what fidelity means to a young man whose hormones are on fire. Right, you get the picture. For most guys, it's all about conquering as many conquests as he can. Granted, there are some that just don't play that game, but you can't bet your life on who's real and who isn't. The best way to protect your self is to protect yourself. There is no sex in this world that feels better than sex with a clean bill of health. Below is a list of STD's and STI's, and a bit of information about both. In addition to reading this, you may want to Google pics of genital warts and genital herpes, AIDS, etc, with your parent or guardian's permission of course (where applicable). If you are lesbian, you are not excluded from this list. According to WebMd.com, "Lesbian women are at risk for many of the same STD's as heterosexual women. Lesbian women can transmit STD's to each other through skin-to-skin contact, mucosal contact, vaginal fluids, and menstrual blood. Sharing sex toys is another method of transmitting STD's. These are common STD's that can be passed between women." Below are 12 good reasons not to have unprotected sex. If you have any of the signs or symptoms, see your doctor immediately. If you do not want any of the signs and symptoms, practice abstinence or safe sex. I know that is so much easier said than done for those of you that are sexually active; you believe this guy and feel that he is completely faithful to you. Chances are that he isn't and your life is in danger. Below is only consolidated info on STD's and STI's. If you want more info, Google the name of the disease or infection for more in-depth information.

- **HEPATITIS B**

SYMPTOMS: Pain in the abdomen, fatigue, dark urine, itching, yellow skin and eyes

TRANSMISSION METHOD: By exposure of infected body fluids.

TREATMENT: (Pre) Preventable vaccine available. (Post) Treatable by a medical professional.

- **HEPATITIS C**

SYMPTOMS: May not have any symptoms, but if symptoms are present, they could include depression, weight loss, yellowing of the eyes and skin, and fluid in the abdomen.

TRANSMISSION METHOD: Contact with contaminated blood.

TREATMENT: Anti-viral drug, liver transplant

NOTE: Can cause liver cancer if left untreated.

- **HIV**

SYMPTOMS: Within a few weeks of transmission, symptoms are flu like and could include, fever, fatigue, sore throat, and flu like symptoms.

TRANSMISSION METHOD: Spreads by sexual contact or contact with contaminated blood, semen, or vaginal fluid.

TREATMENT: Cannot be cured, but treatment may help.

NOTE: HIV is a chronic disease that will cause AIDS if left untreated. No cure exists for AIDS, but strict adherence to anti-retroviral regimens (ARVs) can dramatically slow the disease's progress as well as prevent secondary infections and complications.

- **GONORRHEA**

SYMPTOMS: Women may have lower abdomen pain, men may have testicular pain, but in some cases, there are not any symptoms. Symptoms also include increased vaginal discharge and discharge from penis.

TRANSMISSION METHOD: Unprotected vaginal, anal, or oral sex.

TREATMENT: Antibiotics

NOTE: If left untreated, can cause pelvic inflammatory disease, which causes infertility.

- **CHLAMYDIA**

SYMPTOMS: Eye discharge, pain during sex, discharge from the penis and abnormal discharge from the vagina, and vaginal bleeding.

TRANSMISSION METHOD: Unprotected vaginal, anal, or oral sex.

TREATMENT: Antibiotics

NOTE: If left untreated, can cause pelvic inflammatory disease, which causes infertility.

- **BACTERIAL VAGINOSIS**

SYMPTOMS: May not have symptoms, but if present, symptoms may include itching, foul odor and abnormal discharge.

TRANSMISSION METHOD: It may not be sexually transmitted, as most cases are caused by an overgrowth of normal germs found in the vagina, but having a new or multiple sexual partners may upset the balance of bacteria in the vagina and put you at increased risk.

TREATMENT: Antibiotics

NOTE: You may only have one sexual partner, but your partner may have more.

- **LYMPHOGRANULOMA VENEREUM**

SYMPTOMS: Drainage through skin through lymph nodes on the groin. Painful bowl movements, sores on the vulva or vagina or male genitals, swelling of labia, swollen lymph nodes on one or both sides or in the rectum and bloody stools.

TRANSMISSION METHOD: It's a sexually transmitted bacterial infection caused by three different types (serovars) of chlamydia trachomatis.

TREATMENT: Antibiotics and drainage of the lymph nodes

NOTE: This infection could cause brain inflammation, infection of the heart, eyes or liver, fistulas and narrowing of the rectum.

- **PUBIC "CRABS"/LICE**

SYMPTOMS: Itching in the pubic area, visual confirmation of lice eggs or tiny crabs.

TRANSMISSION METHOD: Contact with the clothing, bedding, towels or pubic region of an infected person.

TREATMENT: There are various over the counter lotions and shampoos available. You will also need to wash your bedding and towels, and follow a very specific protocol to ensure that they have all been eradicated. For more detailed info, please visit http://www.cdc.gov/parasites/lice/pubic/treatment.html

NOTE: Pubic crabs/lice can also take up residence in your eyebrows, eyelashes, armpits or even your scalp, yes, your scalp. I grew up thinking that black people could not get lice, but I stand corrected after visiting www.licedoctors.com/head-lice-and-african-american-hair.html. It states that "No hair is immune to head lice. There is a misconception that African American hair, because it is coarse, is resistant to head lice. Lice do not care whether hair is smooth or coarse, thin or thick. Lice affix themselves to a strand of hair as a way to get up to the scalp to access their food supply: human blood."

- **SCABIES**

SYMPTOMS: Skin rash with red bumps, blisters, relentless itching.

TRANSMISSION METHOD: Sexual contact is the most common form of transmission.

TREATMENT: Oral or topical sabbatical drugs. Over the counter treatments will not work.

NOTE: According to www.medicinenet.com/scabies/article.html, "A severe and relentless itch is the predominant symptom of scabies. Sexual contact is the most common form of transmission among sexually active young people, and scabies has been considered by many to be a sexually transmitted disease (STD), although not all cases are transmitted sexually."

- **SYPHILIS**

SYMPTOMS: Stage 1: Painless sore (3-90 Days after exposure), Stage 2: Body rash (4-10 weeks after initial infection) Stage 3: could affect internal organs (3-15 years after initial infection).

TRANSMISSION METHOD: Sexual contact

TREATMENT: Antibiotics.

NOTE: Could affect internal organs and cause blindness if left undetected.

- **TRICHOMONIASIS**

SYMPTOMS: Abdominal pain, cervix inflammation, vaginal discharge, vaginal itching, irritation and/or inflammation. Foul smelling discharge, vulval inflammation and pain during sex, and/or urination.

TRANSMISSION METHOD: Sexual contact

TREATMENT: Both partners are administered an oral antibiotic.

NOTE: If you have more than one partner, this could be embarrassing. If he has more than one partner, it could come back to visit more often than you planned.

- **CHANCHROID**

SYMPTOMS: Painful, open sores on the genitals, swollen or tender lymph nodes in the groin area, painful urination, and/or defecation, and vaginal discharge.
TRANSMISSION METHOD: Sexual contact

TREATMENT: Antibiotic therapy

NOTE: Not common in women, but not impossible.

- **HUMAN PAPILLOMAVIRUS**

SYMPTOMS: Most people don't have symptoms although some have itching, and/or genital warts.

TRANSMISSION: Sexual contact

TREATMENT: There is no cure for the virus, but the warts can be managed with topical treatments, or they might even disappear. If left untreated, HPV could turn into cervical cancer. If caught in time, several procedures can be performed to decrease the risk of getting cancer. The treatments include the use of a wire loop heated by electric current, to remove abnormal cells, freezing the cells or a biopsy.

NOTE: Not knowing is a dangerous position to put your future self in.

8. NO MEANS NO!

As mentioned earlier in this chapter, if you are a child, no one should be touching your vagina but you, when you use the restroom, bathe or feel the need to explore. If you are a pre-teen and older, in theory, all you should have to say is "no" to hinder unwanted sexual advances, but when your "no" falls on deaf ears, focus on remembering what you are reading at this very moment. Your main goal is to remain safe. If you have been abducted, try your best to remember everything that you can about your surroundings and your abductor so that you can share that information with law enforcement authorities. If you see or hear anyone that could be within earshot of your screams for help, scream as loud as you can and make noises to alert help. However, if you are held at knife or gunpoint and your survival depends on your silence, comply with the demands until you see a clearer path to safety.

Writing this was so hard because it's hard to tell someone to lay there and comply, but STAYING ALIVE IS WHAT YOU WERE BORN FOR. On the other end of the spectrum, fighting as hard and barbarically as you can is the only option. When you come out on the other side of this, you need to see a doctor. Of course, that's a hard idea to fathom - having more strangers in your personal space after such a horrible ordeal, but imagine that the information you provide could potentially save the lives of other young ladies just like you. It is not your hairstyle, make-up, mini dress or your sexy high heels. Do not ever throw this in the closet with your other mistakes because you feel as if you provoked this sicko's behavior. I don't care if he is rich, poor, famous, an athlete, a pop star, a dog walker, surgeon, astronaut, barista, janitor, father, uncle, cousin or friend. If you say no, he is NOT to cross the line of touching or having sex with you. If you are a child reading this, it's likely because you are sneaking around, your parent or guardian found that you were ready for this information, or your parent or guardian thinks that you can benefit from this book and that it may stop you from going down the wrong path. Or perhaps it's because you lack supervision and can do what you want to do. Either way, my only hope is that each of you reading this understands the depth of the power of your NO. No one can take it from you. Even if they succeed at molesting, fondling, violating or raping you, they still didn't turn your "no" into a "yes". No is still no. I may say this a million times, but if you feel that you have been inappropriately touched, you really need to tell someone. If someone is simulating sex with you (humping, hunching, dry humping or whatever you want to call it) and you are a child and they are not, that is wrong too. Make a vow to yourself to tell someone when you feel that your "no" was ignored. Keep a journal and share it with a trusted adult, even if you are afraid to speak about it openly. Just speak. Never let your voice be silenced.

9. STOP PEER PRESSURE IN IT'S TRACKS

I know how it feels to be pushed into a situation. When I was young, there was this monster of a girl that we will call Kenya. She was faster than a Corvette and hotter than a firecracker. Her parents worked a lot so she often had this beautiful home to herself and she ALWAYS cut school. Everyone would follow behind her because they felt that had to. Kenya was tall, stalky, and menacing. I avoided the question at all costs because my mom normally found out whenever I would do something bad, but finally I received an invitation. She demanded that I go with her and a group of other girls and boys to her house during school hours; I cracked under pressure and cut school. We all went to her house and everything that I heard was true. There was smoking, drinking, and sex. I think that I was in the 7th grade and I was more afraid than I had ever been but I didn't want to spoil the fun with my nervous energy while everyone sat around acting grown so I went outside. I sat on the top step and within minutes, I was exposed. I looked to my left and saw this woman who not only went to my church, but my mom also did her hair. Her first question was "Why aren't you at school?" I ignored her and went back into the house like it wasn't me, but when I got home I had to deal with the wrath of my mom who spanked me and unplugged my phone. The next time Kenya demanded that I go with her, I gave her a stern "no" because I definitely had a better shot at winning in a fight against her than the one with my mom. I was happy to have learned that lesson early on because when I transferred to Frick, I needed to strategize against the sea of peer pressure. After awhile, they stopped asking because they knew that I wouldn't go, do it, or try it. I set a standard for myself and I hope that every young lady reading this does absolutely the same.

Tell yourself this every chance that you get. "I AM WORTH THE WAIT." If you are a virgin, a born-again virgin, or someone weighing her options, it's okay to wait. If the guy you are dating is pressuring you to have sex with him, consider that his longing won't stop just because you give in. There is a high likelihood that he will hunt his next prey after he has conquered you. If you wait, you are more likely to make a balanced choice based on a collection of observations that you made over an extended period of time.

If you are questioning yourself, that is one thing. Go to your quiet place and search until you find the answer or have a long hard discussion with someone that you know will NOT impose their beliefs on you or share your secrets without your permission. As they say in the old school, "Don't force it, just relax and let it flow."

10. YOU WERE HERE FIRST

Your womb is the cradle of humanity. What would you do if you were carrying a cradle of precious cargo? EXACTLY! You would be careful, hold it steady, listen closely, and wouldn't make any sudden moves. Take your time, nurture, protect, feed it the right things, bathe and pamper it. According to Wiki, "Lucy" (the common name of Al-288-1) was discovered in a village in Ethiopia in 1974. If you are wondering what AI-288-1 is, it is several hundred pieces of bone fossils representing 40 percent of the skeleton of a female of the hominin species *Australopithecus afarensis* that was dated 32 billion years ago. THIS, ladies, is evidence that we are the cradles of humanity, and always have been. With that said, what will you do to protect your precious cargo? What will archaeologists discover about you if your remains are discovered in 3.2 million years? Definitely something to think about. Grab your workbook/notebook and reflect on ten things that you learned in this chapter that you will apply to your life.

"If you do not know where you are going, any road can take you there." ~ African Proverb

CHAPTER 6

Jar Of Truth

Okay, I have a project for you. Grab a jar, any jar! These days it's so easy to purchase Mason jars from the grocery or craft store. You will also need colorful paper. Various colors would be great or choose one color if you like, but first, you MUST decorate your jar. I used to have several. One was covered with an old, but very cool sock and I covered another in spray paint and glitter. My absolute favorite jar was covered in flat, deep blue beads that I found on clearance at a craft store. If you don't decorate it you are less likely to display it, and if you don't display it, you are less likely to use it. Each jar should have a tag affixed to the rim or on the top of the jar with words on it. The jars can have various labels/functions, including gratitude, prayers, truth, dreams, or even dares, but people are always most intrigued by the jar of Truth, which is why I thought to share with you. When I was going through one of the roughest periods, I would shake it and pull out one of the tiny folded papers and read the message aloud. All of the words are steeped in truth and are specifically designed for you and your village of impressionable young ladies. We must learn to hold each other accountable and most importantly, embrace the idea of lifting each other up! You can write your own messages, but I have put together my top ten below, designed specifically for the little girl in me and the little girls just like me who might need to be lifted from the depths of sorrow into the promised land. After you make your jar, be sure to share it with those who need it even if that person is you.

1. You are an original. There is no one like you. The curliest hair on your head, the drops of melanin in your skin, the thickness in your lips, and the pride in your stride make you the sweet brown sugar infused magic that you are. Don't ever forget that.

2. Melanin absorbs sun? Now it all makes sense...we are light filled beings whose responsibility is to shine and you are doing a great job at being such a vibrant and beautiful light. Shine on.

3. You are the daughter of Mama Earth so dance like the wind, blaze new paths like fire, and be as fluid as water. It is your birthright!

4. I am here to uplift you, not tear you down. I am here to stand with you, not make you fall. I am here to encourage you, not tell you what you cannot do. I am here to love you, because that what sistahs are for.

5. Black girls rock, but you, you beautiful black girl, rock even harder.

6. We are blood sisters. Not biological, but joined by the spirits of our ancestors to make the best of today and a better tomorrow for generations to come.

7. Black is beautiful and doesn't need to be diluted to be more palatable. Embrace the subtle nuances as well as the big, bold and blaring qualities that make you your beautiful vanilla cream, caramel dream, deep chocolate or in-between self.

8. There is an African proverb that says "If you wish to go fast, go alone. If you want to go far, go together." I am packed and ready to conquer whatever it is that you are going through, would like to achieve, overcome, build or create.

9. Black girls have chocolate, vanilla, cinnamon, caramel, honey, butterscotch, cream, hazelnut, speckled and freckled shades of hue, and yours, my dear, looks perfect on you.

10. Never let the odds, naysayers, bullies, your past, society, your neighborhood, unbelievers, your skin color, your body image, your family history, fear, pessimism or anything else keep you from fulfilling your heart and soul's deepest desires.

"If you educate a man, you educate one individual. If you educate a woman, you educate a family."
~ African proverb

CHAPTER 7

Conversations With Your Future Self

1. HEARTBREAK IS INEVITABLE.

IT WILL HAPPEN TO YOU. When it does, always remember that there is a 99% chance that this guy will be someone that you do not speak to very often, if at all in the future. At this moment you are like "What do you mean 'if at all'? I love him… we are going to get married one day!" *RELAX!!* What you are reading is true. Ask your mom if your dad is the same guy that broke her heart in the 8th grade. Ask your favorite couple if they met each other in elementary or even high school. In fact, take a poll and you just may be further convinced that your heart will heal and you are going to be FINE if you do not let this DEFINE you. It's also super important that you analyze your patterns. If your heart was broken by someone who cheated on you, then you must try at all costs not to make that a pattern. Sharpen your intuition and promise yourself not to settle for less. Settling for less means that you are not getting the very best since that is EXACTLY what you deserve. The popular guy who you like just because he has his own car, dreamy eyes, and a cool sense of style isn't usually synonymous with being the best boyfriend, and really, those things will change over the years. But a person with integrity, a good moral compass, character, and a great sense of humor are the only guys that you should entertain.

2. BE THE BEST YOU, FOR US.

Always remember that everything that you do now will affect your life later. Look around you and be thankful of the life that you have, no matter where you are. Please be thankful because there is always someone worse off than you. Now, close your eyes and imagine the life that you want to live. Some of you will envision mansions, but remember that money cannot hold you tight when you are cold or take care of you when you are sick. Completely understanding this may take some time but that is OK, you will get it one day, but the sooner you get it the better off you will be. Consider all of the things that you do today that will affect you tomorrow. It's all about choices.

*   What you choose to eat.

*   What you choose to drink.

*   What you choose to read.

*   What you choose NOT to read.

*   What and who you choose to support.

*   What and who you chose NOT to support.

*   What you choose to do in elementary, middle, and high school.

*   What you choose NOT to do in elementary, middle, and high school.

*   What you choose to advocate.

*   What you choose NOT to advocate.

*   Who you choose to support.

*   Who you choose NOT to support.

*   Who you choose to love.

*   Who you choose to hate.

*   What you choose to say.

*   What you choose NOT to say.

*   Who or what you choose to believe in.

*   What you choose to spend your money on.

*   What you decide is important or not important to you.

I could literally go on and on for days, but hopefully you get the point that life is about choices. Let me rephrase that. You will undoubtedly get the point that life is about choices, but it is my hope that you "get it" sooner than later. The easy choice isn't always the best choice and the best choice is usually not easy.

3. WAITING EXPOSES CLARITY THAT HASTE WILL NEVER SEE.

Point, blank, PERIOD. My father always reminded me to slow down and recognize when God is trying to direct me out of harm's way. My mother taught me that the reward of patience is truth. They were both right! Sometimes I didn't listen and the end result was NEVER favorable. Patience is truly a virtue, young lady, and I know that we live in a "right now" society, but you are the Queen of your Universe and abide by your own rules. Do not let anyone convince you that NOW is the only time to do something that you are not sure about. Waiting gives you a perspective that you will never see if you don't wait. For instance, if you meet a guy and you two become intimate right away and you end up with a broken heart or worse, a sexually transmitted disease, you have yourself to blame for not waiting. Some say that recommending abstinence is an old school way of thinking, but guess what? I don't care what "some people" say and neither should you. Some people will advise the polar opposite of my recommendation and that is exactly why you should make up your mind and stick to it, even if you have already had sex before. It's never too late to wait. If you are considering having sex, WAIT! Grab your notebook and write down the pros and cons of having sex. The pros won't take long and the cons can go on for eternity. Trust me, I remember my mom telling me how important it was to wait for marriage and I registered that idea, but not well enough. I didn't wait for marriage but if I had, I would have saved myself from so much heartache that waiting would have saved me from, so let it save you from that heartache. If you are being pressured to have sex, talk to an adult that you trust about it.

4. GO THE EXTRA MILE BECAUSE "JUST ENOUGH" IS NEVER ENOUGH.

You can apply this theory to almost everything in life and it will not return to you void. My mom always talks about moving from Birmingham, Alabama to Oakland, California. She and my dad were in their early 20's and I was 3 years old. We moved in with my dad's sister (Auntie Frankie), her husband (Uncle Boobie) and their five children, so things were tight to say the least. Four adults and six children in a three-bedroom house wasn't ideal, but my mom's main goal was to make the transition seamless for everyone. She woke up before everyone and cooked breakfast and was the last to go to bed, making sure the house was spotless after she cooked dinner at night. My aunt said that it was one of the easiest times of her life and my mom was showing her gratitude the only way that she knew. She and my dad were not in the position to contribute financially, initially, so she made up for it the best that she could. Another example is when I lost a ton of weight in 2009, my then trainer, Linda, gave me a weekly target to hit that included cardio and fat burning exercises and a two-tier menu that included my basic menu and my extra challenge menu. The basic menu would guarantee that I lost the customary 1-2 pounds per week, but the extra challenging menu was stripped of any rewards. No peanut butter on a rice cake, no brown rice, no salt. It literally included oatmeal and egg whites post workout, and four other meals three hours apart that consisted of four ounces of protein without salt, and asparagus. When I did that, I lost double the weight. It was so hard, but the end result was that I looked and felt better than ever.

In life, going the extra mile includes charity and giving back. Feeding the homeless, offering your services as a tutor or mentor to underprivileged or challenged children, taking out your elderly neighbor's trash are all examples of going the extra mile and in my opinion, it's necessary for character building, but only go the extra the mile in the name of goodness. Going the extra mile to gain something from someone else defeats the purpose. Go the extra mile because it will make YOU better. Go the extra mile because it will make someone's life easier who deserves it. The world needs more of this; it's a good thing you are here.

5. DON'T WASTE YOUR TIME.

The sooner you learn this, the better you will be. I was unhappily married for 12 years. I didn't leave him sooner because optimism got in the way of reality. No matter how optimistic I was, he was going to do the things that ended our marriage anyway. When I finally realized this, a lifetime had passed. DO NOT LET THIS HAPPEN TO YOU! I have also wasted lots of time trying to love people that don't want to be loved, both professionally and personally. I am in the music industry and to be honest, it's slim pickings out here for good people. Most will knock down a group of blind children to get a number one record. Needless to say, I wasted my time trying to make those friendships work. I am guilty of focusing on what people say and not what they do, and this has proven to be a thorn in my side. Put armor on your sides so thorns cannot penetrate. I have listened to people say, "If you do this for me right now because I don't have it, I will repay you when I get in a better place." Guess what? The better place comes and those people will ride smooth past you in their brand new whip, up the hill to their brand new house while you are still at the bus stop picking the dust and lint from your dollar store lipstick. Instead, reach out to God, the universe, or whatever you connect to as the highest power and ask for guidance and protection from people that will use you up until there is a drought inside of your soul. If you ask yourself, "Am I wasting my time?" you are less likely to waste it. This by no means gives you a license to give up on people or projects that you've started. Always honor your word, but know when your time has been spent.

6. TAKE CARE OF YOURSELF.

This seems like a "Well, duh?" moment, but really, ladies. Take care of yourselves from the hair on your head all the way down to your pinky toes, and everything else in between. This includes taking care of yourself mentally and emotionally, as well as physically. There is an interesting article on www.mic.com entitled "6 Actual Facts Show Why Mental Health is an Issue In The Black Community". Some of the highlights of the article include the startling finding by the American Psychiatric Association that states "As many as 1 in 4 adults in the US will suffer from some kind of mental disorder each year and African Americans are at least as likely to suffer from mental health issues as their white counter parts." Each year? Yes, each year. That's why it's important to know yourself and know your body so that you can tell your doctor about changes that you have noticed. It also states that black people heavily use prayer to cope with stress and mental illness and I know that to be true because I have seen it in many families, including my own; God didn't make psychologists and psychiatrists for decoration. He made them as a way to our wellness, so we have to obliterate that stigma. Mental health issues plague every family! We always call the person who is clearly mentally challenged "special". We put them on our prayer lists and jokingly refer to them as our crazy uncle, aunt, or cousin. As a result, we are dealing with an influx of suicides and mentally charged violent events and we can't always change our family's stance on this, but we can start with us. When you have a chance, check out the informative article, https:// mic.com/articles/113030/6-actual-facts-show-why-mental-health-is-an-issue-in-the-black-community#.1BOxRVJwS .

In addition to taking care of your mind, you have got to take care of your body. You only get one. This is one of my biggest regrets because the older you get, the harder it is to lose weight, but it's always super easy putting it on. I talk about weight and health issues so much in this book because it's a demon that I am constantly fighting and I can only hope that you will take my word for it. If you are overweight, lose it. It will eventually affect your self-esteem, your joints, your heart, lungs, bones, and all sorts of other things. There is no food that tastes better than being fit, but I understand how much easier said than done this truly is. All that I can say is try. I hated P.E. class because I have always enjoyed sitting down with a pen and a blank book and writing and I am so grateful for this gift, but I wish that I would have fully committed to everything thrown at me in that class. It's too late for me to start over, but it's not too late for you to take full advantage of the free gym (my description of school). Drink lots of water, take care of your skin. Don't drink sodas. Recognize addictive behavior when you are young and talk to someone about it. Take care of your heart, both literally and figuratively. Wash your sheets every week, if you can. Pray and connect to the highest power in this universe, daily. You will thank yourself for ALL of this, later.

7. SEE THIS BEAUTIFUL WORLD.

I haven't traveled nearly as much as I would like to but my passport is open and ready for stamping. If only I would have thought of this way when I was younger; and that is yet another thing that inspired me to write this book. I hope that someone reads it right now and says, "I'm going to start saving up for Africa now!" I was in my early thirties when I first traveled abroad, first to Italy then on to France followed by a short stay in England. My eyes were fixed open on all of the beauty in front of me: the tapestries at the Vatican and the ruins co-existing with modern architecture in Rome. It was breathtaking and my only regret is that I didn't see it sooner. I was always tethered to a relationship and/or the recording studio, but hindsight is 20/20. I now know that my songwriting would have benefited from my travels and if my relationship couldn't survive me being gone for a month, or even a year, then it wasn't right for me in the first place. If you don't have money to travel, there are options. Start by traveling the World Wide Web via google earth and visit your dream destination, learn the language and develop a plan that will take you there. The plan must include saving money and tapping into every viable resource available. You are free to go and are not confined to the inner city or suburbs. You are and truly free to see this beautiful world!

8. KNOW WHERE YOU COME FROM.

Some of you are foster children or have other family or home-life experiences, so asking your parents questions may not always be a feasible task but knowing where you come from in the broader sense is knowledge that you can seek in the library, on the internet, or even as a result of engaging in conversation with individuals that are knowledgeable about black history. Do you know how long black people have been here in the United States? Do you know when slavery started? Can you name at least five African tribes? If not, study this informative article on http://answersafrica.com/african-tribes.html and when you are finished, be sure to pass the information on to someone else that does not know. The more you know, the more effective you can be at defending your rights, and the more prepared you can be at facing certain issues that only someone like your mother went through when she was your age. If you were raised by your Mother, ask her questions, especially questions about her pregnancy, hair, skin, ailments, her parents...whatever she will talk about, listen. The same goes for your father, extended family, and grandparents. When I was a kid, we would plop down on the floor at my grandmother's house and ask questions about the people in the photo albums, but "actual" photographs are becoming as scarce as "actual" handwritten letters. Remember those? With that in mind, we don't want a similar thing to happen with the rich history planted deep inside of all of us. We need to keep our legacies alive, but to even know the legacy; you MUST ask questions. If you aren't getting along well with your mom, ask her questions anyway. This may be just what your relationship needs. Another side note: if you are at odds with your mom or whoever raised you including an adopted parent, grandma, dad or an extended family member, always remember that things usually change for the better. The older you get, the better your relationship will get, so keep that in mind. Parent/child relationships get particularly rough during the teen years, but time normally heals even the worst relationships. With that in mind, be gentle with the ones that love you and listen to their stories intently, and maybe one day you will share them with your own children.

9. LET LOVE LEAD!

If love is leading the way, you will never be a bully, a liar, a cheater, a racist, an opportunist, thief, or anything that doesn't derive from love. I know that sounds like someone who is literally floating on a cloud and walking on sunshine, but it can be you too. This is something that I recently started applying to my daily life and believe me, it can be a bit of a challenge here and there, but keeping LOVE at the forefront of your brain, on the tip of your tongue, and as your own personal GPS, is life changing. By letting love lead, I crush my ego almost daily. I ask myself, is this done in love? If the answer is no, I don't do it. Well, there are things like paying bills and parking tickets …those are not necessarily done in love but even then, I am grateful for the means to be able to pay bills and I express that gratitude audibly to my personal power source, Jesus Christ. Love comes in so many different colors, shapes, sizes, signs, wonders, and my daily goal is to let that light shine through me and to harness the energy inside of love and spread it around like a wild fire. Love doesn't oppress. Love isn't judgmental. Love doesn't ostracize, love doesn't humiliate. Love isn't violent. Love does not hate. If you want to let love lead, wake up and put it on before your feet even hit the ground. Let it lead your thoughts, your passions, and your choices, then watch what happens.

10. YOU ARE GOING TO BE OK IF YOU...

- Stay in school and get the best grades possible; you may get a scholarship to college.
- Follow your passion, work will not feel like work.
- Vow to yourself to stay away from anyone that threatens to be or is physically violent to you.
- Never believe the man that says he will never hit you again.
- Believe in yourself. Try it, it's contagious!
- Celebrate other women instead of being jealous of them.
- Dance like nobody's watching, even if they are.
- After every time someone breaks your heart, you learn from it.
- Smile at other women and maybe even compliment them when they walk by instead of looking them up and down.
- Give, not just monetarily, when possible and/or help someone that can never help you in return.
- Give yourself breast exams and stay committed to your annual exams.
- Take the stairs sometimes instead of the elevator.
- Stay connected with friends that knew you 'back when'.
- Be fearless and Jump even if you are scared.
- Share wisdom with others.
- Are the voice of the voiceless.
- If you let love lead.

CHAPTER 8

What She Said...

Grab your blank books, girls, because class is in session. It was hard to find just ten quotes for you. Not just ten quotes, but ten life changing quotes spoken by beautiful black women and young ladies who were once girls just like you or are girls like you. To make sure that you understand the quotes, categorize your questions just as they are below and leave LOTS of space between "A", "B" and "C". In the space following "A", explain the quote in your own words. In the space following "B", write how this quote can make a positive impact in your life or in the lives of others and finally in the space following "C", spill your heart out. What does it mean to you? I've completed #1 as an example.

"When someone shows you who they are for the first time, believe them."

Oprah Winfrey

A. *When someone has been fake the entire time and you see his or her true character for the first time, believe what you see.*

B. *I can bring this quote to life in my life by making conscious choices of who I allow to occupy my space after trust has been broken.*

C. *It does not necessarily mean that I need to alienate myself from everyone that hurts me, but making a mental note of one's behavior is always a good idea. Writing it down may even be a good idea too, because it's harder to compartmentalize things that are in bold print, right in front of your eyes.*

"Stay true to yourself and never let anyone distract you from your goals."

First Lady Michelle Obama

"It can be really discouraging to see how far we still have to go and how much work still needs to be done before we can create a world where we're all judged by how we are and not how we look, but I'm strengthened every day because I'm still here, I'm surviving, and I'm using my voice."

Amandla Stenberg

"I am no longer accepting the things that I cannot change. I am changing the things that I cannot accept."

Dr. Angela Davis

"Everyone's got some greatness in them... but in order to really mine it, you have to own it. You have to believe it."

Shonda Rhimes

"If you get, give. If you learn, teach."

Maya Angelou

"I didn't have the confidence I have during my teenage years. But over time you evolve and become really, really comfortable with who you are. Don't apologize for it! Stand firm and stay consistent."

Solange Knowles

"You have to learn how to get up from the table when love is no longer being served."

Nina Simone

"Create the world you want, and fill it with the opportunities that matter to you. Do not let others limit your power."

Alicia Keys

"I hope that my presence on your screen and my face in magazines may lead you young girls on a beautiful journey. That you will feel the validation of your external beauty, but also get to the deeper business of being beautiful inside."

Lupita Nyong'o

"If you want to move mountains tomorrow, you must start by lifting stones today" ~African proverb

CHAPTER 9

Our World! Your Choice! Your Voice!

1. BELIEVE. BECOME.

This is one of the most important things for you to remember because the sooner you grasp this concept, the sooner you will become your best self, even if you ARE 10 years old. Even if you are in high school, college, in your 20's or 30's, in that 44-64 group or even if you are a senior citizen, it is not too late to change your thoughts because when you change your thoughts, everything changes. As a child, my favorite book was The Little Engine that Could. If you are not familiar with the book or the story, please read it and apply the engine's optimism and tenacity to your own life, because the future needs you. After you read the book, write a quick note to yourself about what the book represents, followed by what you will say to yourself to get over whatever hurdle you are facing. For instance, I am going to write, "I will be physically fit", because that is the hurdle at my door. I need to lose weight, period. What hurdle is at your door? What are you stepping over every day? It could be as trivial as a spelling quiz or as serious as cancer. Whatever it is, only plant seeds in your mind that you want to grow.

2. YOUR BODY IS NOBODY'S BUT YOURS!

Your body is yours and as long as you are of sound mind, no one else should be able to take ownership of it. No one should be able to tell you what to do and what not to do with it. It's yours, but always remember that you only get one so never make a quick decision on something that could change the landscape of your body forever. This goes for both the external and internal body. Handle it with care and always remember that NO ONE ELSE CAN DO THIS FOR YOU.

3. VOTE LIKE YOUR LIFE DEPENDS ON IT.

If you are in school, get familiar with the voting process now and as soon as you turn 18, register to vote. In fact, parents, I urge you to include partially filled voter registrations in your daughter's 18th birthday cards! It's that important because we have faced and will likely continue to face double the challenges due to being black and being women. We will continue to face that sad reality if we sit at home thinking "my vote doesn't count", because it *does*. It's your vote that changes the face of Congress, the Senate, and even the White House, to faces that belong to highly capable women that look just like you and me. You must vote because even when women like Ida B. Wells fought alongside her white colleagues for equal rights effecting monumental change in 1920, it wasn't until the 1960's that black people, including a great number of black women, were actually able to vote. You should vote because our ancestors fought for our right to be able to do so. Voting for president is essential, but equally important are your local and state votes. Pay attention to anything that marginalizes women or discriminates against any group of people. Life is too short and love is too long for hate, intolerance, and inequality. Demand that as many people as possible grasp the concept of that principal, because our lives truly depend on it.

If we look into the television's reflection and can't see ourselves, then how will the youth know that it's possible for us to be "there". Seeing Mrs. Obama in the White House is a seed in some little girl's mind reading this right now who could likely be the first black female president. We need those sorts of visuals at the ground level too. If a black woman is a high-ranking political leader, then she can surely be the president of a Fortune 500 company. If a black woman can be a leading surgeon, then a chemistry student is surely capable of getting funded for a life saving AIDS or cancer vaccine. In order to change the narrative, we need to be in the book. Some men still see us as their insubordinates. We need to make equality as clear as glass. It starts with your voice, your vote, and it's your responsibility to uplift other women just like you. We now have a President that condones grabbing us by a word that I don't even have time for, especially in regard to us. We need the White House to be clear, a transparent place that works for the good of everyone in this country and the ONLY way that we can do that is to vote us in. To be clear, "Us" is anyone that believes in and stands for racial and gender equality, social justice, and everything else righteous. #VoteUsIn

4. YOUR SPIRIT.

Your spirit, soul, energy, or whatever you so choose to call it belongs to you and only you. No one can tell you whom to worship, whom to follow, how to find your own personal inner peace and most of all, no woman or man on God's green earth has the right to judge you. As a child, your parents or guardian may take you to church every Sunday, but as an adult, your spirituality is in your own hands. Always be careful not to discredit those who have different views than yours; the spirit is so vast, wide, and deep that the viewpoints will be too many to count, so stand firm in your own beliefs and steer far and clear from anything or anyone that encourages you to engage in any behavior, spiritual or otherwise, that goes against your core values or aims to cause harm to others. I am a Christian who keeps it simple, follows the Ten Commandments, steers clear of judgment, and I try my best to be my best. Once your mind, body, and spirit get in sync, it's really a beautiful thing.

5. ALWAYS RAISE YOUR VOICE.

Stand up for what you believe in. I am sure that I have said that in several different ways throughout this book, but if you don't, who else will? If you believe in something that could make the life of someone else, or even yourself, that much more fulfilled, then why not use your voice to make that change? Your voice may not always be in the form of protest or social media rants, either. It may be your mere presence, an email pointing out an injustice or your name being associated with a specific charity. Whatever it is, don't be quiet about it. Speak up for you. Speak up for us. Speak up for your ancestors who were beaten, raped, and kept from learning to read as well as the ancestors that were college educated, traveled abroad, became doctors and adorned the beautiful pages in our history books. Ooh, in fact, let's fast forward to forty years from now. You are reading an excerpt about you in a history book. What does it say? Grab your notebook and let your imagination and your future voice align.

6. BE CERTAIN OF THE COMPANY YOU KEEP.

"I can't be framed if I am not in the picture" is one of my favorite quotes. It is to the point and truer than true. If you hang out with girls that fight all of the time, you have an increased risk of getting into a fight yourself. If you spend your time around people that believe they are not going anywhere, then there is a strong likelihood that you will end up at the same destination, so guard your space. My mom always said, "Association brings out assimilation" and although I rolled my eyes, it seems like perfectly good advice now but the consequences are far worse than what they used to be, so I am hoping that you grasp this concept without actually having to assimilate some terrible behavior and pay with consequences. Another cliché that I find to be true is "show me your friends and I will show you your life." You may think that you are polar opposites now, but there is definitely something that attracted you to your frenemy, so choose wisely. Stay away from gossipers, haters, jealous people, bullies, and anyone that deep down you know will do the same to you that they are doing with you. Good friends may sometimes only mean just one, but that's okay. Quality over quantity every time.

7. YOUR SEXUALITY.

Just like with your body, mind, and spirit, your sexuality is yours alone. You should never feel threatened or hushed. You should be able to walk tall in your truth without judgment and you should never be faced with violence if someone disagrees with your sexuality. If you are in school and someone needs to be reported, the code to the streets ends here for us...tell someone. Hold people accountable for the mean things that they say, look them in the eye and affirm your beliefs without blinking. Even if tears fall, stand firm. If your voice shakes, stand firm. Widen your eyes and stare the fear inside of them down so hard that it cowers and runs away. You are here because you deserve to be, just like everyone else. Don't let someone else's hatred seep inside of you, having you thinking the unthinkable. Instead, think about how much of a difference your voice will make and start speaking up. Never even for a moment should you consider ending your own life because of your sexual preferences.

8. MAKE SURE YOU DO SOMETHING THAT YOU LOVE FOR A LIVING.

Starting now, write down your top three preferred professions. Watch the list Starting now, write down your top three preferred professions. Watch the list change over the years. If you are retired or already have a profession and it's not your passion, write down your top three passions in your notebook. This exercise is important in helping you keep in touch with your dreams. The 405 freeway doesn't only suck because of traffic, but sometimes when I am on it I look over at the driver next to me and they look innately unhappy, on average. Not the kind of "oh, traffic sucks" unhappy, but just really deeply unhappy. My guess is that a great deal of people are indeed unhappy, but you don't have to be. You can find out if you are living by your passion by writing down your five favorite things to do, things that you would do for free, excluding things for family and faith. Mine are below.

1. Music

2. Writing

3. Cooking

4. Helping People

5. Movies

These things have not changed much for me over the years, and although being self-employed can be quite the challenge sometimes, I am very happy that I am living by passion. One of my best friends, Delanie, loves arts and crafts and she is an art director, creating and overseeing new and innovative craft projects, daily. One of my longest, dearest and best friends since 5th grade, Kyra, wanted to see the world and couldn't be happier being a flight attendant. What couldn't you be happier doing? Write it down and never forget it. Your life depends on it.

9. INSPIRE AND/OR MENTOR AS MANY PEOPLE AS YOU CAN.

Imagine that you never were inspired by anyone in this world. Hard to imagine, right? In fact, it's nearly impossible. Some people may not have people that inspire them in their own families but connecting with someone, be it a teacher, mentor, or even someone from afar is the only way that we know. Now that you know that, it's your responsibility to inspire. It's your responsibility to share, mentor, and teach others what you know. If you want to be or would like to connect with a mentor, please contact http://www.bbbs.org/site/c.9iILI3NGKhK6F/b.5962335/k.BE16/Home.html for a wealth of information, but don't forget that you can inspire someone right now. How? Tutor, run for student government, share your story with someone that needs to hear it, show someone the ropes. Be an inspiration by doing well in school, excelling at your job, being a good daughter, sister, mother, cousin, friend. Be an inspiration by defying incredible odds but always remember that this information does NOTHING while lying dormant inside of you. It needs to get out and be infectious. Let it. In the interim, please grab your notebooks and write down ways that you can mentor and/or inspire someone right now, then do it. I have to add that I have mentored with the Spark program for two years now and my heart is overflowing with love and gratitude for this program and my mentees, Simone and Jimena. Spark formed a partnership with AMAPS and thanks goodness for that because it's been reciprocal. Sure, I teach the girls things, especially Simone who has been with me since day one, but I learn from them too. Simone is so light hearted and optimistic and has taught me to always look for the sunshine, even on days that look like night. Thank you, Simone. If you are interested in connecting with Spark, the offer mentorships in various parts of the US, so please visit www.SparkProgram. Org for more information.

10. GIVE BACK.

This is an extension of #9, yet entirely different. Giving back is even more selfless. The hungry do not care if you want to be the next Oprah, you can't inspire them in that way. All that they want to do is eat and when you are blessed enough to give back, you feed them. Sometimes you will be an inspiration, and other times you will be the girl scooping out the mashed potatoes; either way, give with your heart. When you outgrow your clothes and if your parents don't have plans for them, give them away. Organize a drive at your school to help children in your community. If you have a talent, you can give back with that too. Play your guitar and sing a song at the hospital on a Friday night instead of getting into trouble. Volunteer to read to children at the library or walk dogs at the shelter. There is so much that needs to be done. Pick up trash in your neighborhood or create a website that causes others to give back in ways only you have imagined, but always keep in mind that "giving" is selfless. Don't do it for money, accolades, social media likes or status, or else it isn't 'giving' anyway. Give with a pure heart while wanting nothing in return. Your notebook should still be nearby. Write down ten ways that you plan to give back and give yourself ten years to follow through on all of them. Then ten years from that date, repeat. It's my hope that you create a cycle of giving that changes and enriches many lives, including your own.

"If you close your eyes to facts, you will learn through accidents." ~ African proverb

CHAPTER 10

The B.G.P. (Black Girl Pledge)

Put your right fist in the air and your left hand behind your back or on your hip. With your feet spread shoulder width apart, fix your mind's eye on your dreams, your desires, passions, family, your people, and yourself. Focus on the goodness that love and life have to offer as you firmly state the words below:

Every morning when I wake, I will tell myself that I am healthy, **smart**, **successful** and **beautiful**, conditioning my mind to **think the very best of me**. I will **walk boldly** in my **blackness** and will NEVER shrink or minimize myself to fit into anyone's box. I will **listen** intently to **both** the **wise** and the **foolish**, learning from their **victories** and **mistakes**. I will do more than just my part; I will go **above** and **beyond**, **wide** and **far**, but NEVER beneath, or intentionally at the detriment of another to get the results that I want out of life. I will always do my best to be a resource for my sisters and a light source for humanity. I embrace every curve on my body, every kink in my hair, and every drop of melanin in my hue. I am proud to be a black girl (or woman) and will always stand in solidarity with the righteous. I will change the world, starting with my own. I will encourage my brothers to be the Kings that they are, and will stand beside them in the face of adversity. I will use my voice to echo the cries of the voiceless and demand necessary change. I will keep the spirit of my ancestors alive, sharing my rich history and legacies with the world at large, but especially at home with my family. I am fully aware that my future is already a seed firmly planted in my mind, and my beliefs will become my harvest, therefore I will water it daily with love, positivity, kindness, strength, and good intentions. I will become what I believe, good or bad, so I believe that I am good. I believe that I am smart. I believe that I can change the world. I believe that I am capable of doing anything that I put my mind to. I believe that I am healthy. I believe that I am a pillar of strength. I believe that to love and to be loved is my birthright. I believe that if I lead with love, love will follow, and it is so because _____(insert your name) says it is.

If you think you are too small to make a difference, you haven't spent a night with a mosquito. ~ African Proverb

Acknowledgements and Thanks

I could never have written this book if it weren't for the mighty village that raised me, and the queen of that village is my mom, Yvonne Stinson. Mom, thank you for allowing me the freedom to be me. You always supported me and never discouraged me from following my dreams. In fact, you are the one that watered the seed of creativity that had no choice but to blossom! Thank you for STILL relentlessly encouraging me and for being my loudest and sometimes only cheerleader, even in the face of "eventually" and "maybe next time". You always helped me to find the YES hidden in the haystack of NO's. I love you so much, thank you! You are one of a kind and I am so glad that you are my Mother.

Dad, thank you for being the change that I needed to see, a pillar of strength, and a sounding board that never echoed my cries to anyone else but God. Thank you for your endless prayers and for still calling this grown woman your Baby Girl. I can't wait to share your triumphant "Sinner to Saint" story with the world. You are such an amazing person and I am so glad that you are my Father.

Thank you, Tanecia and Glen. I love you both. Tanecia, thank you for unknowingly inspiring me to write this book throughout your life. You are literally the new and improved version of me and you make me excited for the legacy that will be carried forward. I love you so much.

Grandma Grace, at 87 years old, you are still the brightest flame. Thank you for laying our foundation. I love talking to you about the old days, while learning so much about myself at the same time. Thank you also to my family. My aunts

(Trisha, Sandra (Robert), Faye, Kandi, Charmelle, Shug, Frankie (Rev. McCurdy), Donna (Leonard), and Ella Mae) and Uncles (Mike M. (Cheryl), Danny (Trish Ann), Jit (Pat), Mike S (Lenna), Cedric (Patrcia) and Ronnie), and my cousins (too many to name all of you, but especially my bruzzin Daryl and my suzzins Nadia, Phaydra, Joya and her husband Billie Chavarin, Mariah, Aaron, Wendy, Nykia, Nard, Treasa, Lil Mike, Marcus, Tony, Nard, Rell and Lil Mike). Also, my 'framily' – those friends whose blood seemingly runs through my veins and includes those that have been there every step of the way, as well as those who I don't speak to often, but when we do we don't skip a beat. I love you Kyra Dyas & The Dyas Family, Darien Dorsey & the Dorsey Family, Raphael Saadiq & Family, Candace Coles, Logan Coles, Peyton Coles & The Coles Family, Adama Wilson & The Wilson Family, Charles & Quiana Kelley, Delanie West & Family, Tiffany Villarreal & P, Roxanne Ross & The Ross Family, Brely Evans Eddings & the Evans Family, Carol Ware & Mark Ware, Ron Dyer (thanks for being such a great friend to my mom), Chrissy & Rodrigo, Major, Jamie & Mya Hawkins, Doobie Powell, The McElhaney's, Keyshia Cole & DJ, Nioshi Jackson, Mykah Montgomery, Odessa Donovan, Alexis Cornn, Tia, Pastors Charles & Andrea Humphrey, Joi Gilliam & Keepy, Monet & Kai Owens & Family, Angie Warner, BJ, Gregory & Justice, Jai & Tasha & St. Cyr Family, Shari & Shannon Watson, Justin Merrill, Omega Brooks, Dottie, Alayna, Stephanie, Michelle Lochin & Family, Keyshia Cole & DJ, Marcus King, Charlez, N'dambi Gillespie, Gillian Ovid, Ledisi Young, Quin, Aria & Addision, Nicole, Simone, Chad, Adam & Shani, Andre Benjamin, Adam Woss, Todd Shaw, Damone Roberts, Vichelle, Monica Payne, Amber Bullock, Shawn Barton, Yanory Silva & Family and Tash Jennigs. If I have forgotten anyone…I got you on the reprint :) I am so blessed to have all of you in my life!

Thank you to Adah Glenn for your amazing artwork for this book and Stacey Debono for superb editing as well as being the first person to read this book and give me so much encouragement with your kind words. My deepest gratitude also goes to my Insta cousin and dear friend, Shawanna Davis for seeing my vision and deciding to JUMP in, regardless of an enormously full plate. Also, thanks to Matthew Moses for holding the pieces together and to my team, Shamari Hartzog and my first cousin, Aaron Grayson for every single brick that was laid by you all! Many thanks to Jared and Julia at Wildbound PR for getting the word out too.

Boundless thanks to my music publisher, Andy McQueen, for always believing in me and never giving up on my vision. I also thank Wendy Goldstein and Maya Drexler for inspiring me to breathe life into this project in a way that I hadn't considered before.

Thanks in advance to anyone that has read this book. Please spread the word in any way that you can.

Resource Center

The Resource Center is filled mostly with invaluable links that will be of a great help to you. If you do not have access to a computer, please visit your local library. Most of them have computers with internet access. In addition, some schools allow students to access computers, as well as local colleges, churches, and community centers. I designed the Resource Center to be accessible via the internet because it really opens doors to an entirely new world. With the internet, you are just one click away from discovering a whole world, and I encourage you to discover it. Not the seedy gossip sites that we are all guilty of falling captive to, but for instance, Google Earth can take your eyes on a journey started in your mind. It's all about visualization so once you see Table Mountain in South Africa and visualize yourself at the top, maybe you will be more likely to go there. I know that I will. I know that I'm talking about it like it's a new invention, but the world wide web really is fascinating and I urge you to explore it in a way that you haven't before, starting with this Resource Center. Follow the links by typing them manually, or go to my website and copy and paste them into your browser and off you go. Even if you have not purchased the book, the resource links are available to everyone. Please keep in mind that informative links are blue, but links that require action are green. For instance, below Oral Care, the CDC link will lead you to the aforementioned link that I referenced earlier in the book, but the green link will require further action. In this case, the link for Obama Health Care is useful if you do not have a health or dental plan. The rest is self-explanatory. If you have any trouble, please feel free to drop me a line and I will try my best to get back to you. Happy surfing, girls.

BLACK HISTORY

AFRICAN TRIBES

http://answersafrica.com/african-tribes.html

http://www.gateway-africa.com/tribe/

http://www.africanbookscollective.com/books/the-ways-of-the-tribe

https://en.wikipedia.org/wiki/List_of_ethnic_groups_of_Africa

https://www.africaguide.com/culture/tribes.htm

AFRICAN PROVERBS

http://www.wow4u.com/african-proverbs/

https://twitter.com/africanproverbs

http://www.nairaland.com/1891848/funny-wise-african-proverbs

http://www.afriprov.org/images/afriprov/books/bassaintro.pdf

www.siliconafrica.com/100-african-proverbs-i-always-keep-with-myself/

HISTORY

www.PushBlack.org

travel.allwomenstalk.com/ancient-tribes-of-africa

www.gpb.org/Black/History

https://blackamericaweb.com/category/little-known-black-history-facts/

http://www.blackfacts.com

www.kulturezone.com

http://oyc.yale.edu/african-american-studies/afam-162

http://blackhistoryclass.blogspot.com

http://www.theroot.com/slavery-by-the-numbers-1790874492

http://www.pbs.org/wnet/african-americans-many-rivers-to-cross/

www.anikefoundation.org

https://www.youtube.com/watch?v=5oL8A9NwU1c

http://www.pbs.org/show/africas-great-civilizations/

www.blackhistory.eb.com

www.raaheroes.com

https://www.africa.com/many-african-languages/

http://www.royalty.nu/Africa/

100 Best Websites for African Americans

http://www.dcwatch.com/iilist/100best.htm

BULLYING AND CYBER BULLYING

Crisis Call Center   800-273-8255   (or text ANSWER to 839863)

24/7

http://crisiscallcenter.org/crisisservices.html

CyberTipline   800-843-5678   24/7

http://www.cybertipline.com

Your Life Iowa: Bullying Support and Suicide Prevention
(855) 581-8111 (24/7) or text TALK to 85511 (4pm – 8pm everyday)
Chat is available Mon – Thurs 7:30pm – 12am

http://www.yourlifeiowa.org

www.standforthesilent.org/

https://blackamericaweb.com/2012/05/29/bullying-among-the-very-young/

CANCER

THE SISTERS NETWORK has countless resources designed specifically for US including "The Sister House" which is a home away from home for Breast Cancer patients and their families that are receiving treatment. In addition, they offer a program called BCAP (BREAST CANCER ASSISTANCE PROGRAM). Please visit their site! Even if you are a college student, they have resources for you that are certain to keep you on track . If you would simply like to answer the soul call to pay it forward, please follow the green link to volunteer.

www.SistersNetworkInc.org   http://register.sistersnetworkinc.org

Minority Health Resource Center	www.omhrc.com
Lung Cancer and African Americans	http://www.stopcancerfund.org/p-lung-cancer/lung-cancer-and-african-americans/
Cancer causing carcinogens	http://www.cancer.org/cancer/cancercauses/othercarcinogens/athome/antiperspirants-and-breast-cancer-risk

CHEMICALS TO AVOID

https://www.collective-evolution.com/2012/04/10/you-have-the-right-to-know-17-chemicals-to-avoid-in-cosmetic-and-personal-care-products/

http://blackgirllonghair.com/2012/02/5-chemicals-to-be-mindful-of/

https://blackliberationlovenunity.wordpress.com/2015/05/07/9-reasons-to-avoid-perms-and-relaxers/

https://docakilah.wordpress.com/2013/01/07/the-dangerous-effects-of-perms-hair-relaxers/

https://blackliberationlovenunity.wordpress.com/2015/05/07/9-reasons-to-avoid-perms-and-relaxers/

http://www.huffingtonpost.com/vanessa-cunningham/dangerous-beauty-products_b_4168587.html

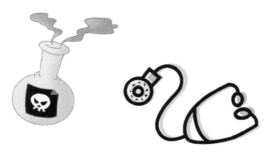

COLLEGE GRANTS & SCHOLARSHIPS

http://www.collegescholarships.org/resc_minority.html

https://www.goodcall.com/scholarships/female/african-american/

http://blackstudents.blacknews.com

https://www.scholarships.com/financial-aid/college-scholarships/scholarships-by-type/minority-scholarships/african-american-scholarships/

http://www.scholarshipsforwomen.net/african-american/

200 Free Scholarships for minorities!

http://www.blackexcel.org/200-Scholarships.html

http://www.studentgrants.org/african-american/

https://colleges.niche.com/scholarships/race/african-american/?source=f

http://sites.ed.gov/whhbcu/2013/11/21/scholarship-opportunities-for-minority-students/

http://www.collegescholarships.org/grants/women.htm

http://4blackyouth.com/scholarships.aspx?id=minority

http://collegebound.org/scholarships-internships/

http://hbculifestyle.com/101-minority-scholarships/

http://www.gograd.org/financial-aid/scholarships/women/

http://www.collegegrants.org/eyes-on-the-college-prize-grants-for-african-american-students.html

http://www.bestcolleges.com/financial-aid/minority-students/#african-american

https://www.salliemae.com/plan-for-college/scholarships/minority-scholarships/african-ameri

Black Girls Rocking College

http://www.clutchmagonline.com/2014/02/know-black-women-lead-groups-college-enrollment-watch/

DEPRESSION

Crisis Call Center
800-273-8255
(or text ANSWER to 839863)
24/7

http://crisiscallcenter.org/crisisservices.html

National Hopeline Network
800-SUICIDE (784-2433)
800-442-HOPE (4673)
24/7

http://www.hopeline.com

http://www.blackwomenshealth.com/blog/black-women-and-mental-health/

DOLLS AND TOYS

http://www.naturalgirlsunited.com/natural-hair-dolls.html

https://www.etsy.com/shop/LeenGreenBean

http://www.ashtondrake.com/mcategory/child-dolls_8343/african-american.html?
ipp=36&cm_ven=GPS&cm_cat=Google%7CSearch&cm_pla=Dolls%20-%20Affinity%7CAfrican
%20American%20Child%20Dolls&cm_ite=african%20american%20child%20doll%7Cb
%7CProduct&gclid=CP-z0KLcuM4CFUGUfgodvdUHjQ

https://www.google.com/#q=black+dolls&tbm=shop&spd=4453200502062422394

http://www.ethidolls.com/gallery.html

http://www.walmart.com/ip/39878920?
wmlspartner=wlpa&adid=22222222227030196346&wl0=&wl1=g&wl2=c&wl3=50700614432&wl
4=pla-
103257791312&wl5=9031186&wl6=&wl7=&wl8=&wl9=pla&wl10=8175035&wl11=online&wl12=
39878920&wl13=&veh=sem

https://www.etsy.com/listing/379123687/african-doll?utm_campaign=shopping_us_c-
toys_and_games-toys-
dolls_and_action_figures_osa&utm_medium=cpc&utm_source=google&utm_item=0&utm
_ag=27087759547&gclid=CM3gv4fduM4CFZFffgodWC0Awg

https://www.facebook.com/naturallyperfectdolls

http://www.uzurikidkidz.com

http://atthewellconferences.org

http://hiatoys.com

https://www.alibaba.com/product-detail/hot-selling-wholesale-black-dolls-
life_60134452936.html

http://www.4kidslikeme.com/brands/Melissa-and-Doug.html

https://www.browngirlsclub.com/collections/party-supplies

https://www.browngirlsclub.com/collections/pillows

https://shop.indegoafrica.org/pages/wholesale?gclid=CjsKDwjw6qnJBRDpoonDwLSe ZhIkAIpTR8J_BE5dZ5lGjiogKDzRlNanA_ZMBucot4U00GNXORWvGgI5I_D_BwE

https://www.etsy.com/listing/488593743/dark-skin-tone-superhero-favor?ga_ order=most_relevant&ga_search_type=all&ga_view_type=gallery&ga_search_ query=african%20american%20themed%20party%20supplies&ref=sc_gallery_3&plkey= bba494f33791193a53d4c2076a23b87fcbed6ea6:488593743

https://www.etsy.com/listing/493161268/spa-themed-zebra-print-african- american?ga_order=most_relevant&ga_search_type=all&ga_view_type=gallery&ga_ search_query=african%20american%20themed%20party%20supplies&ref=sr_gallery_16

https://www.etsy.com/listing/268383783/african-american-girls-spa-party-favor?ga_ order=most_relevant&ga_search_type=all&ga_view_type=gallery&ga_search_ query=african%20american%20themed%20party%20supplies&ref=sr_gallery_17

https://www.etsy.com/listing/474482763/girl-superhero-cupcake-toppers-african?ga_ order=most_relevant&ga_search_type=all&ga_view_type=gallery&ga_search_ query=african%20american%20themed%20party%20supplies&ref=sr_gallery_36

Dolls, Bedding and Party Supplies!
http://www.uzurikidkidz.com

EATING DISORDERS

Crisis Call Center
800-273-8255
(or text ANSWER to 839863)
24/7

http://crisiscallcenter.org/crisisservices.html

National Association of
Anorexia Nervosa and Eating
Disorders
630-577-1330
10am – 6pm EST, Mon – Fri

http://www.anad.org

National Eating Disorders
Association
800-931-2237
9am – 5pm, EST, Mon – Fri

http://www.nationaleatingdisorders.org

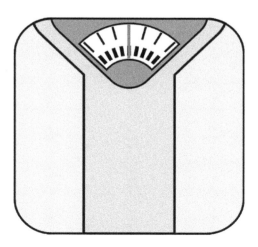

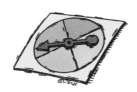

EDUCATIONAL GAMES

http://www.orientaltrading.com/web/browse/processProductsCatalog?
Nrpp=10000&sku=13630271&BP=PS519&ms=search&source=google&cm_mmc=Google-_-
242030648-_-20452920848-_-Black+History+Flash+Cards&cm_mmca1=OTC
%2BPLAs&cm_mmca2=GooglePLAs&cm_mmca3=PS519&cm_mmca4=FSANY&cm_mmca5=S
hopping&cm_mmca6=PLAs&cm_mmc10=Shopping&cm_mmca11=13630271&cm_mmca12=Bl
ack+History+Flash+Cards&gclid=CKrLkLn6uc4CFZKCfgodOKoLUg&categoryId=377320&Nrpp
=10000

https://www.etsy.com/listing/226398677/black-history-month-bingo-game-60-cards?
utm_source=google&utm_medium=cpc&utm_campaign=shopping_us_e-
paper_and_party_supplies-other&utm_custom1=e179963a-28ae-4ac5-8603-
06f09084af95&gclid=CKiy6df6uc4CFRSPfgodAn4C1w

http://www.itsablackthang.com/collections/african-american-board-games

GRIEF AND LOSS

Crisis Call Center
800-273-8255
(or text ANSWER to 839863)
24/7

http://crisiscallcenter.org/crisisservices.html

Tragedy Assistance Program
for Survivors (TAPS)
800-959-TAPS (8277)
24/7

http://www.taps.org

National Hopeline Network
800-SUICIDE (784-2433)
800-442-HOPE (4673)
24/7

http://www.hopeline.com

HAND WASHING

http://www.cdc.gov/handwashing/why-handwashing.html

HEART DISEASE

Go RED for Women	https://www.goredforwomen.org/about-heart-disease/facts_about_heart_disease_in_women-sub-category/african-american-women/
Self Check	https://selfchec.org/self-checks/heart-diseases/?utm_term=%2Bhow%20%2Bto%20%2Bprevent%20%2Bheart%20%2Bdisease&utm_content=Heart%20Disease%20Prevention
Dangers of Cigarette Smoking – How you think you look vs How you REALLY look	http://www.cdc.gov/tobacco/campaign/tips/resources/data/cigarette-smoking-in-united-states.html?gclid=CjwKEAjw_oK4BRDym-SDq-aczicSJAC7UVRtpsgIB2vqdAnURn44jWS3SelRGjACLxKaln2sK7VBERoCU0fw_wcB
Matters of The Heart	http://www.bwhi.org/issues-and-resources/heart-disease-and-black-women-the-silent-killer-that-speaks-volumes/

HIV

http://www.thebody.com/content/46201/hivaids-resource-center-for-african-americans.html

http://www.cdc.gov/hiv/group/gender/women/

https://www.ncbi.nlm.nih.gov/pmc/articles/PMC2831751/

https://www.dailychargeapp.com/?utm_medium=cpc&utm_campaign=HIV+App&utm_content=HIV+App&utm_term=hiv+positive+resources&moc=0622000100&utm_source=google&gclid=CPnWsaK1lNQCFe0RfwodIH8BRw&gclsrc=ds

http://www.thewellproject.org/?gclid=CjsKDwjw6qnJBRDpoonDwLSeZhIkAIpTR8KTVm7wDtdg6yYncnBguSRRwaw-HveAoDnblQ0Byk8uGgL2pvD_BwE

http://magicjohnson.org/programs/hivaids-initiatives/

https://www.prezcobix.com/living-with-hiv/glossary?&utm_source=google&utm_medium=cpc&utm_campaign=PCX+DTC+-+HIV+General&utm_content=HIV+General+-+General&utm_term=hiv&gclid=CJG40t-1lNQCFVNVfgodIJYK_w&gclsrc=ds

http://www.peerstrong.com/?gclid=CjsKDwjw6qnJBRDpoonDwLSeZhIkAIpTR8JW3KMnp71hFjcURENruswiXf01VBHQ_6Yhnsn--qVhGgJYafD_BwE

Homelessness & Runaways

http://www.blackandmissinginc.com/cdad/safety.htm

http://nationalsafeplace.org

Crisis Call Center 800-273-8255 (or text ANSWER to 839863)   24/7

http://crisiscallcenter.org/crisisservices.html

Boys Town National Hotline – serving all at-risk teens and children 800-448-3000 24/7

http://www.boystown.org/hotline

National Runaway Switchboard 800-RUNAWAY (786-2929) 24/7

http://www.1800runaway.org

Thursday's Child National Youth Advocacy Hotline 800-USA-KIDS (800-872-5437) 24/7

http://www.thursdayschild.org

<u>MENSTRUAL HEALTH</u>

http://teenhealthsource.com/puberty/periods/

http://www.amightygirl.com/blog?p=11614

MENTAL HEALTH CRISIS

National Mental Health
Association Hotline
800-273-TALK (8255)
24/7

http://www.nmha.org

National Institute of Mental
Health Information Center
866-615-6464
8am – 8pm EST, Mon – Fri

http://www.nimh.nih.gov/site-info/contact-nimh.shtml

Thursday's Child National
Youth Advocacy Hotline
800-USA-KIDS (800-872-5437)
24/7

http://www.thursdayschild.org

https://mic.com/articles/113030/6-actual-facts-show-why-mental-health-is-an-issue-in-the-black-community#.1BOxRVJwS

http://ourselvesblack.com/links/

http://www.ebony.com/life/black-mental-health-resources#axzz4iRUvHQX1

https://thisismybrave.org/resources/

http://mhaac.org/support/mental-health-resources/community-mental-health-resources.html

http://www.stevefund.org

https://minorityhealth.hhs.gov/omh/browse.aspx?lvl=4&lvlid=24

http://www.letserasethestigma.com/african-american-mental-health/

MENTORING/DEVELOPMENT PROGRAMS

www.BlackGirlsRockInc.com
www.BCWNetwork.com
www.blackwomensblueprint.org
http://www.suwn.org/how-you-can-join-us?gclid=CPTJ3ryIus4CFUGSfgodZrMG4g#mentor
www.NationalCongressBW.org
www.ncnw.org
http://www.liveyourdream.org
www.BlackGirlsCode.com
www.BlackGirlsSmile.org
www.100blackwomen.org
www.bwhi.org
www.nawc.org

http://www.womenlikeusfoundation.org/one-girl-at-a-time-1/
http://www.daysforgirls.org

Big Brothers and Sisters of America
http://www.bbbs.org/site/c.9iILI3NGKhK6F/b.5962335/k.BE16/Home.htm

www.sparkprogram.org/

ORAL HYGIENE

http://www.mouthhealthy.org/en/az-topics/o/oral-health

http://www.webmd.com/oral-health/features/eight-ways-to-keep-your-mouth-healthy

http://www.cdc.gov/oralhealth/oral_health_disparities/index.htm

http://www.obamacareplans.com/get-quotes/?
CID=28458&SRC=op_google&bw_state=0&bw_type=0&bw_brand=0&Sub_ID=
%2Bobamacare&bw_keyword=
%2Bobamacare&google_network=g&creativeid=86424640382&position=1t2&matchtype=b&m
obile=

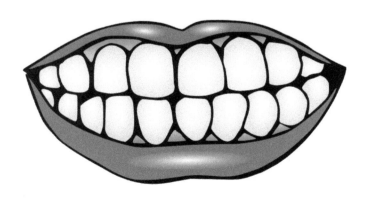

RAPE, SEXUAL AND DOMESTIC ABUSE

Crisis Call Center
800-273-8255
(or text ANSWER to 839863)
24/7

http://crisiscallcenter.org/crisisservices.html

loveisrespect/ National Teen
Dating Abuse Helpline
(866) 331-9474
24/7

http://www.loveisrespect.org

National Domestic Violence
Hotline
800-799-SAFE (7233)
24/7

http://www.ndvh.org

Rape, Abuse, and Incest
Network
800-656-HOPE (4673)
24/7

http://www.rainn.org

Safe Horizons Rape, Sexual
Assault and Incest Hotline
Domestic Violence Hotline –
800-621-HOPE (4673)
Crime Victims Hotline – 866-
689-HELP (4357)
Rape, Sexual Assault and
Incest Hotline – 212-227-3000
 TDD for all hotlines – 866-
604-5350
 24/7

http://www.safehorizon.org

REGIONAL

ALABAMA (Birmingham) http://www.thissistercares.org

CALIFORNIA (Los Angeles)
http://www.sparkprogram.org/index.php/get_involved/volunteer?gclid=CNWtneGlus4CFc1lfgodjCQOPg
www.GirlsClubLa.org
www.BWWLA.org
www.latm.org/
https://www.suwn.org/

CALIFORNIA (Oakland/Bay Area)
http://www.sparkprogram.org/index.php/get_involved/volunteer?gclid=CNWtneGlus4CFc1lfgodjCQOPg
http://www.cinnamongirl.org
www.girlsinc-alameda.org
http://igniteca.org/
www.jloeb.org

GEORGIA (Atlanta) www.leadingladiesatl.com

ILLINOIS (Chicago)
http://www.sparkprogram.org/index.php/get_involved/volunteer?gclid=CNWtneGlus4CFc1lfgodjCQOPg
http://www.commongroundfoundation.org
www.flowersinbloom.webs.com
www.shesallthatfan.com
http://polishedpebbles.com

KENTUCKY (Florence) www.youngpearls.org

MARYLAND (Baltimore)
http://www.flygirlnetwork.org
http://www.dreamgirlsmentoring.org
http://www.sisterscircle.org

MARYLAND (Glen Dale) www.alegacyleftbehind.or

MICHIGAN (Dearborn Heights) — www.truebelles.us

MISSISSIPPI (Hattiesburg) — www.kuntrykidzinc.org

NEBRASKA (Omaha) — www.reconnectsuccess.com

NEW JERSEY (Newark) — www.girlslivelovelaugh.org

NEW YORK (Bronx) — www.theblackpearlprogram.com

PENNSYLVANIA (Harrisburg) — www.jelanigirlsinc.org
PENNSYLVANIA (Philadelphia) — http://www.sparkprogram.org/index.php/get_involved/volunt eer?gclid=CNWtneGlus4CFc1lfgodjCQOPg

RHODE ISLAND — http://ncbwri.org

SOUTH CAROLINA (Sumter) — www.princessnme.org

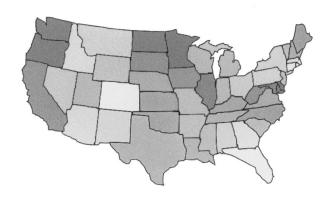

SCHOOL VIOLENCE

Crisis Call Center
800-273-8255
(or text ANSWER to 839863)
24/7

http://crisiscallcenter.org/crisisservices.html

National Center for Mental
Health Promotion and Youth
Violence Prevention

http://www.promoteprevent.org

Speak Up
866-SPEAK-UP (773-2587)
24/7

http://www.bradycampaign.org/our-impact/campaigns/speak-up

Thursday's Child National
Youth Advocacy Hotline
800-USA-KIDS (800-872-5437)
24/7

http://www.thursdayschild.org/

Sex Trafficking

https://rights4girls.org/wp-content/uploads/r4g/2015/02/Af-Am-Girls-Trafficking-July-2016.pdf

SEXUALITY & SEXUAL HEALTH

American Sexual Health
Association
919-361-8488   http://www.ashastd.org
8am – 8pm EST, Mon – Fri

Centers for Disease Center
(CDC) Info
800-CDC-INFO (232-4636)   http://www.cdc.gov
24/7

Crisis Call Center
800-273-8255
(or text ANSWER to 839863)   http://crisiscallcenter.org/crisisservices.html
24/7

GLBT National Youth Talkline
800-246-PRIDE (7743)
4pm-12am EST, Mon – Fri and   http://www.glnh.org/talkline
12pm – 5pm EST Sat

Planned Parenthood National
Hotline
800-230-PLAN (7526)   http://www.plannedparenthood.org
for routing to local resources
24/7

Thursday's Child National
Youth Advocacy Hotline
800-USA-KIDS (800-872-5437)   http://www.thursdayschild.org
24/7

TransLifeline
US – 877-565-8860
Canada – 877-330-6366   http://www.translifeline.org
24/7

https://www.google.com/#q=hepatitis+symptoms
http://www.cdc.gov/parasites/lice/pubic/gen_info/faqs.html
www.medicinenet.com/scabies/article.htm
https://www.google.com/#q=syphilis
https://www.google.com/#q=Trichomoniasis
http://www.cdc.gov/std/tg2015/chancroid.htm

https://www.google.com/#q=chancroid+symptoms
https://www.google.com/#q=human+papillomavirus+infection+symptoms
http://umm.edu/health/medical/ency/articles/lymphogranuloma-venereum

SKIN CARE

http://madamenoire.com/270203/15-of-the-best-foods-for-clear-skin/

SLEEP & REST

http://www.sleephealthjournal.org/article/S2352-7218%2815%2900015-7/fulltext

SUBSTANCE AND ALCOHOL ABUSE

Crisis Call Center
800-273-8255
(or text ANSWER to 839863)
24/7

http://crisiscallcenter.org/crisisservices.html

Thursday's Child National
Youth Advocacy Hotline
800-USA-KIDS (800-872-5437)
24/7

http://www.thursdayschild.org

The National Alcohol and
Substance Abuse Information
Center
800-784-6776
24/7

http://www.addictioncareoptions.com

SUICIDE

National Suicide Hotline
800-SUICIDE (784-2433)
800-442-HOPE (4673)
24/7

http://www.hopeline.com

National Suicide Prevention
Lifeline
800-273-TALK (8255)
24/7

http://www.suicidepreventionlifeline.org

The Trevor Lifeline (US Only)
866-4-TREVOR (488-7386)
24/7

http://www.thetrevorproject.org

Your Life Iowa: Bullying
Support and Suicide
Prevention
(855) 581-8111 (24/7) or text
TALK to 85511 (4pm – 8pm
everyday)
Chat is available Mon – Thurs
7:30pm – 12am

http://www.yourlifeiowa.org

http://www.sprc.org/sites/sprc.org/files/library/Blacks%20Sheet%20August%2028%202013%20Final.pdf
http://thinkprogress.org/health/2016/02/22/3750881/black-youth-suicide/

TAXES / IRS

https://apps.irs.gov/app/understandingTaxes/student/hows.jsp
https://apps.irs.gov/app/understandingTaxes/student/simulations.jsp
https://www.irs.gov/individuals
https://apps.irs.gov/app/understandingTaxes/student/tax_tutorials.jsp

TEEN HEALTH

http://www.teenhealthandwellness.com/static/hotlines
http://www.huffingtonpost.com/glenn-d-braunstein-md/early-puberty_b_1826072.html

TEEN PREGNANCY AND PARENTING

Abortion Information and Resources

http://www.arhp.org/Publications-and-Resources/Patient-Resources/Fact-Sheets/Early-Abortion

Baby Safe Haven
Confidential Hotline – 888-510-BABY (2229)
Safe Haven Infant Protection Laws enable a person to give up an unwanted infant anonymously without fear of arrest or prosecution as long as the baby has not been abused.

http://safehaven.tv/states

Boys Town National Hotline – serving all at-risk teens and children
800-448-3000
24/7

http://www.parenting.org

Postpartum Support International
800-944-4PPD (4773)
Calls returned within 24 hours

http://postpartum.net

American Pregnancy Helpline
866-942-6466
24/7

http://www.thehelpline.org

Birthright International
800-550-4900
24/7

http://www.birthright.org

Crisis Call Center
800-273-8255
(or text ANSWER to 839863)
24/7

http://crisiscallcenter.org/crisisservices.html

Planned Parenthood National
Hotline
800-230-PLAN (7526) for
routing to local resources
24/7

http://www.plannedparenthood.org

Thursday's Child National
Youth Advocacy Hotline
800-USA-KIDS (800-872-5437)
24/7

http://www.thursdayschild.org

Statistics

https://www.americanprogress.org/issues/race/report/2013/11/07/79165/fact-sheet-the-state-of-african-american-women-in-the-united-states/

www.hhs.gov/adolescent/teen-pregnancy

http://www.ncsl.org/research/health/teen-pregnancy-affects-graduation-rates-postcard.aspx

http://lisdemo.libguides.com/c.php?g=425586

VAGINAL HEALTH

https://www.verywell.com/
http://www.cosmopolitan.com/health-fitness/advice/g2720/vaginal-odor/
http://www.medic8.com/healthguide/vaginosis/what-is-bacterial-vaginosis.html
http://www.wikihow.com/Get-Rid-of-Vaginal-Odor-Fast
http://teens.webmd.com/girls-puberty-10/puberty-changing-body
https://en.wikipedia.org/wiki/Labia_minora
https://en.wikipedia.org/wiki/Labia_majora
https://en.wikipedia.org/wiki/Clitoris#Glans_and_body

VOTING

Voting Rights

https://www.nwhm.org/online-exhibits/rightsforwomen/AfricanAmericanwomen.html

Voter Registration

https://www.rockthevote.com/register-to-vote/?source=cagoogle&gclid=CjwKEAjwrcC9BRC2v5rjyvSbhWASJACKkjDz1blxnwjlNjQSiKwjQY_UoujTAxwL2rJDfX91OYlyExoC7MPw_wcB

https://www.vote.org/am-i-registered-to-vote/?gclid=CjwKEAjwrcC9BRC2v5rjyvSbhWASJACKkjDzCdDKOxthux-Av2c8W1RX5wXfY8RVinhmmwtewXGdjhoCQ3Hw_wcB

About The Author

Taura Stinson was born in Birmingham, Alabama and raised in Oakland, California where she first started as a songwriter and penned the first release for a then unknown girl group from Texas called Destiny's Child. Since then, she has written songs for various artists including Jennifer Hudson, Mary J. Blige, Steven Tyler (Aerosmith), Raphael Saadiq, and Usher. Stinson also co-wrote the Grammy nominated songs *Show Me the Way* for Earth Wind & Fire and *Good Man* for Raphael Saadiq, on which she was featured.

In addition, she works as an independent music executive, garnering a Grammy win for her first project, *The Awakening of LeAndria Johnson* from BET's Sunday Best, and as a background vocalist while a member of the Bang-Bang Girls who have recorded background vocals for Stevie Wonder, Jesse J, Ariana Grande, Mark E. Bassy and Tori Kelly. She currently lives in Los Angeles and is a voting member of both the Grammy's and the Academy for Recording Arts & Sciences. Find out more about Taura, or make contact through her websiteTauraStinson.com